BEYOND THE Credentials.!?

By Evans Kwesi Mensah

ISBN: 978-1-7325517-4-9

Printed in the United States of America

PRAISE FOR BEYOND THE CREDENTIALS!?

B eyond the Credentials is amazing and is definitely an inspiring book. It is riveting and provides powerful guides for those whose dreams of a successful life have been stalled. The book offers great insights on how to navigate the professional world. It provides strategic advice and concrete examples on how best to succeed not only in our professional careers, but also in our daily lives. The book contains something for everyone. Read this book and your life will be changed forever.

Dr. Jean-Marie Jean-Pierre
Ph.D., MBA, NASCOM Service Integration Program Director, NASA Goddard Space Flight Center, Code 770, Mission Networks Division

---

Mensah says: "networks can open doors, but knowledge sustains you". His book, *Beyond the Credentials* is a practical guide to business success. It tackles topics such as family life, good values and ethics, faith, health and friends. Each section includes a worksheet. Other topics include: diversity, culture, communication, and reputational capital. Many will see this work as a leadership book, but I think it is advice for successful living. I highly recommend it.

Professor Kip Wotkyns
Professor of Journalism and Media Production, Metropolitan State University, USA; Graduate of both Columbia and Stanford University; Former reporter for FORTUNE magazine and a copy editor for TIME magazine; Former president of Leman Publications Inc. A licensed remote pilot airman

---

In an age of unprecedented uncertainty, this book reminds us of the power of relationships and the importance of maximizing work-life-education opportunities, while maintaining balance. Evans provides a manifesto through storytelling of his life as a husband, businessman, father, scholar, son, friend and colleague. The format of short chapters—ranging from relationships, reputation and mindset to ethics, cultural awareness and goal setting—includes worksheets. The book is useful to anyone looking for a guide to improve their networking skills, while being mindful and present in their life.

Professor Sandy Zook, Ph.D.
Assistant Professor, School of Public Affairs, University of Colorado, U.S.A.

In *Beyond the Credentials*, author Evans Kwesi Mensah discusses the tension that exists between educational attainment and family life. He argues that although educational attainment and professional success are salient aspects of an individual's life, neglecting family life could come at a huge cost. He emphasizes the importance of a strong marriage and a resilient, doting relationship with progeny as essential to becoming a well-rounded individual. These values, as he calls them, go beyond monetary or superficial success; they engender fulfillment, happiness, and contentment.

The author also addresses the importance of good morals, without which professional success would remain a shallow accomplishment. He argues that "[m]oral decency paves a unique path" for the one who embraces the highest levels of ethicality, as the latter makes it possible to leave ineffaceable footprints in the lives of others.

Addressing the benefits of diversity, the author emphasizes the cognate relationship between success and diversity — the two go together. He argues that society would be improved if we all embraced the smorgasbord of racial, ethnic, religious, and gender differences that exist in America's pluralistic society. No one is an island, and no one can go it alone.

Overall, this timely and important book delivers nuggets of knowledge and wisdom that will serve as a useful guide to the reader for years to come.

I highly recommend this book to the public!

Professor Daniel K. Pryce, Ph.D.
Assistant professor, Department of Sociology & Criminal Justice at Old Dominion University, Norfolk, VA. Author of several scholarly publications on police–immigrant relations, police–citizen relations, and immigration studies.

This book burst off from the belly of the author who uses very practical and many personal experiences to illustrate and drive home his points about the importance of living a life beyond the physically demonstrable. From section to section, the author cautions against "successful failures"—being very successful in one aspect of one's life but being a huge failure in another aspect. Like repeat medication for a chronic disease, I will read it again and again and again and I think many well-suited, lettered and impeccable English-speaking professionals need to read this book to get "saved". There is too much goodness in this single book. Beyond the credentials, our "character"—the total embodiment of who we truly are in all the many life circumstances we find ourselves—will be revealed and will define how we are perceived. This book provides very useful nuggets that EVERYONE requires.

Professor Justice N. Bawole, Ph.D.
Dean, University of Ghana Business School; Ph.D. in Development Policy and Management from the Global Development Institute, University of Manchester, UK. Also, MPhil, BSc. from University of Ghana Business School.

Evans Kwesi Mensah's 2nd book, *Beyond the Credentials*, is once again chock-full of knowledge and essential viewpoints to consider for improving your life's journey. Evans helps readers discover and understand that there is so much that goes on "behind the scenes" that makes life truly fulfilling and worth living. His latest book has a unique way of making the invisible visible.

Evans was sure to include space at the end of each section with key questions to simply guide you on your own personal discovery of how the data may be true for you and how you can apply it in both your personal and professional lives. Dare to take a look and take appropriate actions to help yourself, those close to you, and the world achieve their lives' full potential. Highly recommended!

Ellen Firestone
Chief Operating & Service Officer, Simon Eye, and Founder of thefirestone.org

This one is entirely dedicated to my mother, Rev. Felicia Mawusime Akosua Nyamakade Anyagli-Mensah (Dade), in blessed memory. Without her strong and caring hands (obviously with my father), I would not have been able to reach the height of success that I have. From diapers to degrees, she prepared me well for the world. It's rather sad she isn't alive to see it all unfold. Every good mother should be celebrated!

ACKNOWLEDGEMENTS

To my dearest wife 'Baake', who supported my vision for this project from day one. When you marry your best friend, you support each other's visions, even in difficult times—this is what I have in my wife.

To my boys, Selorm Evans Jr, Selasie Ethan and Sena Eamonn (a.k.a. 'S.J.', 'Papa E', and 'Gergeh', respectively) who, despite their young age, were so passionate to share their ideas— some of which are covered in this book.

Professor Eric Osei-Assibey cannot go without being mentioned. It was a moment during a brief discussion in his office on some of the concepts I already cover in my executive training sessions that sparked the idea for this book.

All who made time to read part or all of the manuscript to assist in the flow of the work, including my endorsers and forwarder, you're one of a kind. For making time for me, you're amazing.

To everyone that encouraged me to release a second book after the successful unleashing of my maiden one which became a bestseller. Especially my cousin Woenya Agbo, who literally professed it to me, but I laughed at the idea. To all of you, here you go! I doubted, but you believed; now here we are! Thank you.

CONTENTS

FOREWORD

In interviewing job candidates or prospective students, I am often asked, "What is the most important thing you are looking for in making a decision?" The answer for me has always been "passion"—whether it be passion for the job the person seeks or the course of study the person intends to pursue. Indeed, it is far easier to coach someone passionate to success—regardless of the person's credentials—than it is to lead someone to success who brings many academic degrees but lacks passion for the job or course of study. A curriculum vitae offers a snapshot into a person's skills and experience, but it is only one piece of information about a candidate. Credentials can certainly matter, however, who you are as a person will always matter most.

I have had the privilege of knowing Evans for more than ten years and during that time his most enduring and steadfast trait has been a desire to elevate others to achieve their own aspirations. In his second book, Evans has encapsulated many keys to success in a series of clear, direct lessons and examples that everyone can easily use to shape their professional and personal path. He carefully avoids using "business speak" and instead focuses on sharing lessons that he has personally experienced and grown from during his own career, which makes for a very pragmatic guide on how to self-assess and take a thoughtful approach to personal and professional development.

This book comes at an important time for all of us to examine the basic principles that bind us together: decency, compassion, thoughtfulness and collaboration in building a better world. Evans' work is a reminder to stay true to core values and realize that credentials are merely one element of who we are, and never the most important.

Beyond the Credentials is an important book in that it will help many people, across many cultures, rethink their personal plans and strategies for building their own path to success. In particular this book is likely to resonate with up-and-coming individuals who are launching their careers or seeking to take their self-reflection and how they present themselves to others to the next level of professionalism. Above all, this book offers a pragmatic set of questions and recommendations for anyone looking for self-improvement and a means of contributing to society—something that is of true lasting value to our shared humanity.

- Jason Rabbino -

EVP & Chief Commercial Officer, Towne Park, New York. Formerly, Group President for Brambles; SVP of Enterprise Sales, Tyco International; Vice President of Strategic Development for Aramark and an Associate Principal with McKinsey & Company.

Jason was an aircraft commander and division officer with the US Navy flying the SH-60B Seahawk aircraft. He is a graduate of both Wharton and George Washington University. He is also a Commodore's List graduate from the US Navy flight school program.

AUTHOR'S 30,000 FOOT PREVIEW

For most of my professional life, rarely do people or institutions inquire about my academic credentials. It is apparent that I certainly do have the necessary degrees and certifications; however, what they are ultimately interested in is my expertise and ability to deliver to their satisfaction. Assuming I could not perform as expected, my credentials would not do the job or cover-up for me. That's why it is said, "networks can open doors, but knowledge sustains you!" There is a dire need to translate degrees into delivery to be that "go-to person."

What does matter in the quality of your work is Results! Results! Results! Results matter a lot in this dynamic, ever-changing world of ours and cannot be replaced by your accolades alone. While you pursue higher titles, accolades and degrees, and other awards (which you should pursue), remember your status can only take you that far. What will help you win that business deal or give you that promotion is the right work ethic. Don't expect to be the glorified "go-to person" simply because of your advanced education alone.

When you're hired into an institution for the first time, almost everyone welcomes you with happiness. They might take you for lunch and even decorate your desk or office with balloons in celebration of your arrival, but that only lasts a short while. When all is said and done and the boss needs that critical work output or report to present to the board, you had better deliver, else your credentials will be questioned, and not even your physical beauty or handsomeness will save you.

Professors, whom I respect a lot, provide the foundational knowledge that college students need to start their careers. After a while, knowledge begins to mean less and less. If students do not build on this foundation with practical experience, they cannot and will not rise above their peers. This practical experience is critical.

Practical business expertise is crucial in these competitive, fast-growing environments. This is the reason institutions invest heavily in recruiting the right talent, occasionally inviting corporate leaders to appear and train college students to attain the heights required by the current market.

This book is targeted to everyone willing to transform their mindset from the status-quo. It is excellent for training and for coaches, professors, students, business leaders, and professionals (young or old, executive or junior, seasoned or new).

And as a final thought and disclaimer to my readers, this book is not in any way looking down on attaining higher academic achievements, accolades, awards, credentials, or titles. If it so suggests, then I look down on myself, because in my humble way, I have achieved quite a few of such recognitions. This is the reason the title of the book is 'beyond,' not 'without.' Instead, my main goal is to educate and to share some critical but necessary ethical nuggets based on a combination of research, observations of what has helped people succeed and fail, as well as my own personal experience. I urge you to read to the very end to see the entire artwork.

–1–

STRONG FAMILY LIFE

Despite your awards, titles, accolades, and wealth, without good family life, all successes and values are worthless. What does it profit a person to gain success, but lose his or her entire family in the process? Your family knows you beyond the credentials. It's important to connect emotionally and to be physically present as well. There's no exception. It's like building a home instead of a house—which is all about your mindset.

A good marriage, loving children (biological or not), friends that become family, good parents, the importance of physical and emotional connections are some of the key factors to consider.

Even if you're single, unearthing the best from your inner being through family relationships is key.

While your colleagues at work may know you as the execution genius or the dealmaker, your family knows you beyond the credentials. All too often, people invest a significant amount of time in sharpening their craft and being the best in their careers. More often than not, family and friends are ignored and or placed on the back burner. What if we flipped that around and invested as much time in the family as we do in our professional development?

Your family knows your achievements, but they also know who you truly are, far more than your colleagues. They know your innermost struggles and your foibles. They play an instrumental part in your success in the corporate world and the world at large. This is why it is so important to invest time and effort in building a strong family, as they provide a strong foundation necessary to build a home. Otherwise, you are just living in a house. One must ensure they are investing valuable time in developing a good marriage, raising respectful children (nieces and nephews alike), and nurturing good friends. Those who are single are no exception, as they may have nieces and nephews who look up to them, and they cannot disappoint them. Each one has a role to play. When this is done well, you can turn your house into a home.

There's an old saying, "blood is thicker than water." It is always believed that those with whom you have biological relations (blood) are dearer or closer to you than a friend (in this case, water). I do not entirely agree with this assertion. In my experience, I have deep ties to my biological family. Still, over the years, in my life's journey and travels around the world, I have personally built and nurtured certain relations that have become more than friends. They became family. My family laid the foundation for me and provided the essentials needed for life survival, but some of my friends have become the umbilical cord to my aspirations.

Yes, a direct family member can be close to you, which is the natural way it is expected to be. However, the depiction of every other relationship aside from those with blood relations, as less valuable, is not accurate in all cases. In my case, some of the people who surround and raise my flag through thick and thin are friends, not necessarily direct family members—though my family also supports me and play their role as expected. Simply put, your credentials, titles, accolades, and all the things you're so proud of are worthless without good friends and close relations.

Whom you marry is important, so choose well! This is the person with whom you will build a home and a future. To build a home and a future, you must invest in it—heavily! I like to think of a good marriage in the same way that I think about the phenomenon of shared dreaming. Shared dreaming occurs when two individuals have the same dream. It is a rare occurrence, but it does happen. One of the key glues in my marriage is effective communication on every subject matter—ranging from business, family, our children, and even silly chats that bring us to serious laughter. While my wife and I have individual aspirations, we also have shared dreams in our relationship—similar to a corporate goal, which we pursue together in order to thrive. Consider two individuals who are so connected and tuned in to one another that they share the same dreams, goals, and vision. This connection is the power in selecting a good spouse and spending time nurturing the relationship. It doesn't mean we don't have our differences, argue or disagree. It also doesn't suggest that it comes easy. My wife and I have had more disagreements than I can count, but what matters is that we see eye to eye on the things that truly matter most. My wife is the number one supporter of my achievements, and the reverse is true too. However, if I did not meet her emotionally and be present physically, nothing would matter more.

My children are all at a young age at the moment and are aware of my failures and successes, but they could care less. Playing catch or going to the playground is more meaningful to them than any accolades, titles, or credentials I could bring home. I like to enjoy playing horse with my children when I am home; it creates a sense of joy when I can get down on their level and be a child again. My youngest enjoys piggy-back rides. Anytime I bend over to pick up something from the floor, he sees it as an invitation to hop on my back. With children, these simple acts matter. They may not remember the color of your suits, all the awards that you have won, or your executive client list. However, they will remember the quality time spent together talking about the things that matter to them, the stories you share, and playtimes. They will more readily recall that you attended their sports event, and musical recital than anything else. They will value the time spent making art and being silly. In the long run, these are the things that matter most!

I must admit, spending time with family at times can feel like a heavy burden. After a long day of work, the last thing you may want is a child jumping on your back. Sometimes your work schedule can conflict with their after-school events. If you work from home (especially with the Corona Virus Pandemic, or COVID-19), business calls can encroach on your family time – especially when you have clients globally. However, spending quality time with family shouldn't cost you too much time; this is time that should be factored into your weekly activity. I do have to make a conscious effort to play with them, even when I'm not in the mood after a long day of work. However, I also find other ways to kill two birds with one stone.

Most times, I make an effort to read with my children. At one point, I would read one story and spend other times sharing ideas in my mind from my first book—at a level they can understand. I used the opportunity to take them on the book-writing journey. During one of our nightly rituals, I shared with them how the ideas we discussed during our book-writing journey were captured in a book that became a best seller.

One day, my middle son went to his teacher and shared, "my daddy is a bestselling author." He encouraged her to look into the book. The teacher took note and researched the information, and when she found out that it was true, she purchased the book on Amazon as a gift for her husband. The teacher sent the book home with my son with a kind note asking for my autograph.

She emailed us regarding this interesting conversation between herself and my son. My wife and I asked our son about it, and he confessed that he did. So funny, he never mentioned it to us earlier. We all laughed over it, but the point here is building a good relationship with your children, nieces, and nephews goes a long way in cementing your future relationships.

My oldest son shares his emotions of admiration by holding and cuddling with a calm tone in his voice, calling your name with special meaning in his eyes and tone. Though he is an outgoing person, when it comes to emotions, he uses gestures a lot—all of which depict our close relationship.

Someone asked a rich man once, "Do you take care of your family and children?" The rich man responded, "Yes, of course! I buy them clothes, I provide a house for them, and I pay the nanny sufficient money to take good care of them." Whoa! Spending money is not sufficient. Your spouse, kids and friends all need your physical presence and emotional connection whenever you can, except during periods like the COVID-19 pandemic when physical distancing (not social) is implemented against its spread. All things equal, not everyone has the same space to be physically present all the time, I get that, but your busy schedule should not also become an excuse for rarely being present. Over the last fourteen years, I learned the importance of these two needs. When it comes to physical presence, the quality of it is important. In my line of business as a global business strategy consultant, I can't be with my family all the time, but I can make sure that the time I do spend with my wife or children or friends is worthwhile and memorable. You will grow emotionally through your attachment to your family. As your children or dependents grow, despite the challenges that come with every stage, emotions grow also.

My parents who planted combinations of discipline, common sense, love for us and others, respect for any human being, and the right education to succeed in life have played their roles in making sure their children were not lost, but gained confidence and then strove to reach the top. One should understand that good teachers, like your parents, sometimes fall short of their own advice, as it was in the case of my parents whose relationship ended in divorce. One cannot deny the investment and impact they made in our lives as children—their sweat, sacrifice, dedication, faith in our success, and pride in us as their children. The onus is on us to do better than them—by making the right choices, not only in marriage but career choices, by appreciating whatever we have in life but not remaining complacent, and by making it to the highest level as far as the color of the blood in our veins remains red.

In a nutshell, if you truly want to have a long-lasting and meaningful family life, invest in your family and friends. Leave your credentials at the door (or the garage) before entering your home.

• Food for thought:

At the end of the day, work hard to support your family, if they depend on you. Balancing work-life calls for providing for the needs of your loved ones—whether married or not. However, if you are married, having a good and productive marriage is essential to your good health, and so it is with spending quality time with your children, nieces, nephews, and loved ones as much as you can. So it is also with a single person who can find his or her joy in close relations as indicated.

Love and respect your family as they go through trials and tribulations. Don't betray those who stood with you in difficult times; don't turn your back on those who once defended you. Some provided a little support here and there for you. They also contributed towards the bridge in your life that led to your big victory today or in the one yet to come. Believe!

The COVID-19 pandemic came to redefine the priorities in our life—FAMILY! It has also come to humble humanity and nations. The virus does not discriminate and fears no one. It is not shy of the color of a person's skin. It is regarded as the 'great neutralizer' of human beings. Coronavirus does not obey anyone, regardless of your position in society. It does not seek permission to operate. The rich and the wealthiest can have it, and so can the poor and the tattered. In fact, it does not consider your titles, accolades or credentials before it operates. What other lessons can we learn from this?

Nature, or whatsoever you may call it, has come to teach mankind lessons through the virus, now that the entire world has been arrested. One thing is clear; everyone was quarantined with their family and loved ones—the first and last resort.

Worksheet:

I talked about my wife and I and how we communicate—though not a perfect relationship. Share the ways in which you relate with your spouse. If you're not married, list a few things crucial to you as far as family life is concerned.

Finally, discuss how you balance family life and children (if any—biological or not) as well as friends and loved ones, considering the personal examples elaborated in the chapter.

_____

_____

_____

_____

_____

_____

_____

_____

_____

_____

_____

_____

_____

-2-

HAVING GOOD VALUES

Values can be things you naturally acquired or were born into, (from family or lineage, etc.) or things you grow to learn and adapt to as part of your life's journey.

Values are what describe and define who you are. They are mostly internal and drive your core beliefs, your actions, your inactions, and the decisions you make daily—which reflect externally. Values serve as your propeller, dictating where you spend your time and energy, the social groups you associate with, and even the things to which you give your attention. They determine what your priorities should be, and, deep down, values can help you evaluate if your life is turning out the way you want it to be. Let's understand that someone else's values may not be yours. What someone believes may be different from what you believe. Not all values may be acceptable—the fact that something is your value does not necessarily mean it is right.

Values are not what you write down (alone), but what you do or do not do. Every institution has mission and value statements. Unfortunately, for some companies, they are simply words written on some document but not lived out. Some institutions, for example, may have rules around protecting the disabled to appease the government, but the work environment does not practice those words. I know some major institutions that have written statements encouraging employees to share their views when they see anything wrong, promising anonymity and protection. Still, in reality, when an employee follows those procedures, they are not protected. These are not the type of values to which we are referring. Values should be followed through with dignity and respect.

Who doesn't want money, happiness, and love? Those things are certainly important, and at their core these are the things that matter and should be considered part of life's ecosystem as ethical values. What do you stand for? What are you known for? What are you recognized by? Values are like having a brand attached to you. They are like being known for a particular skill you possess and keep as your own.

What is your brand? When people look at you, how are you recognized? Values drive your brand, in the sense that people see you and identify with you based on what you portray yourself as in their presence. If you're known to be someone who speaks appropriately all of the time, then all of a sudden you start using foul language, people will look at you with dismay. The reverse is also true, though the change will be seen in a positive light. This is the reason some people can be forgiven for a bad joke, and another person could be alienated by the same joke. Case in point, when a person mentions "Chick-Fil-A" as a fast-food restaurant in the United States, what comes to mind? Even if you have a cursory idea of the company, you know that they are known for excellent quality fresh food. If you visit one of their stores, the experience is incredible! You are treated with dignity and respect as if you are the only customer. The food and service set them apart from other fast-food restaurants. They are known for taking a strong religious stand by NOT opening their chain of restaurants on Sundays due to their Christian beliefs. You don't have to believe what they believe, but because of their values, you know you will always get superior service, at the same time, you know you won't get to buy their food on Sundays. This is true at every chain across the nation.

Just as individuals, families, countries, cultures, and companies have their unique values, so it is with religious or non-religious groups. Taking Muslim and Christian religions, for example, they have strong values against indulging in alcoholic beverages—whether or not this is practiced religiously depends on the individual. However, in their value books, it is a rule of thumb to avoid such alcoholic beverages, if possible. For a Muslim, prayer time is a solemn act; they are supposed to give all their attention to the act of praying. There is no way a phone will ring and he or she will pick it up. This is so true that children learned they could get away with a great deal during prayer time. I recall a story from a Muslim friend who said, when they were young, the only loophole they had to mess around against their mother's wishes was when she was praying. This poor woman would take the chance when she lifted her head to send a message with her eyes telling them to stop what they were doing, but the kids ignored the warning—nothing stopped them. However, immediately when she finished, they would all run away, forgetting they had to return to eat or sleep at home and face whatever punishment was waiting for them.

Catastrophic situations reveal our actual values, and they need to be managed with wisdom. Let's take, for example, if you need to pick your children up from school at a particular time, and there is a disaster in your area which could kill you, why jump into the storm which might kill you before reaching your loving children, instead of waiting until it is safe to do so? This is applying wisdom to what you do. This is in no way tweaking your values and promises but instead, being wise and safe. This will not reduce you, rather prolong your life.

Learning not to compromise on your values calls for focus, determination, and persistence. Learning to say, "no," is a skill set—it is a yes in reverse.

"Have the courage to say no. Have the courage to face the truth. Do the right thing because it is right. These are the magic keys to living your life with integrity."

- W. Clement Stone -

If you do not eat meat for cultural reasons, that becomes your value. If you tell yourself you will not pick up work-related calls when out of the office, that becomes your value to live by. These are values that one can maintain. If, however, one of your beliefs is never to eat meat as indicated, and you find yourself in a jungle, stranded for days and weeks without any possibility of living except to eat what you detest, there is nothing wrong with eating meat to survive.

When you come back to normal life, alive, your values can continue. I do not see this as compromising your values. However, I stand to be corrected, as this is my viewpoint. What one needs to be cautious about is not to make values a 'religion.' Meaning, while it is good to have such values (some are crucial), try to evaluate some of the values based on the situation and make the best possible decision.

On the contrary, if you're a woman and your value is to be chaste till you marry, and you find yourself in a corner where men, for example, are pestering you for sex, you can avoid such advances and make your stand straight to them without trying to be a "King Kong." By this I mean you can withstand any challenge by avoiding taking such an early stance. Many have fallen on the sword for trying to prove a point and never return the same. It all depends on you.

• Food for thought:

Values are essential to have because they serve as guiding principles. They serve as a coach, a teacher, a mirror, and a reminder to you. What are your values?

Worksheet:

What do you consider a good value in your life? List five (5) areas that you consider values which you will not compromise.

_____

_____

_____

_____

_____

_____

_____

_____

_____

_____

_____

_____

_____

_____

_____

_____

_____

_____

-3-

ADDING VALUE TO ONESELF

Movement doesn't always mean progress unless you're adding true and positive value to yourself. You may be counting the grey hairs on your head or yet to, but remember, anytime you visit the salon or the barbershop or desire to shave, it is a sign that you're adding years to your age. Ask yourself, what value am I adding to myself every day as the days go by?

Adding value to oneself may be similar but separate at the same time from having ethical values, as indicated in the previous chapter. One can argue that both are the same, in the sense that adding skills and impacting the way you think and look at things are similar. This manifests itself in how you change to see things around you. In other words, both are internal, and both can be seen through your actions. However, the slight difference left for debate is that, this type of value (adding value to oneself) is geared towards personal development, and it is more outward. At the same time, the former (having good values) is more internal but reflective when exhibited.

When Kobe Bryant joined the NBA Lakers team at age eighteen, his initial plays accumulated many mistakes, lots of air balls and many from the three-point lines. Others like his teammate, Shaquille O'Neil, even his rival and idol, Michael Jordan, and many others, believed in him, and he bet on himself to do well—the rest is history. He had to add value to himself to become valuable and one of the most respected, and arguably one of the greatest NBA players who ever played the game. Kobe Bryant left the game a Laker Legend and scored sixty points, becoming the third-leading scorer in the NBA history until he was passed on the all-time scoring list by LeBron James the last night of his life on earth. As if he knew that was his last night, he tweeted to LeBron, "Continuing to move the game forward @KingJames. Much respect my brother #33644." This is a good reminder that you must live your life to the fullest by having respect and good character alongside.

Adding value to oneself creates opportunities for you which you may not have had under normal circumstances. If you want to marry a prince for example, learn to walk like a princess, talk like a princess, dress like a princess, be around where the princes are, and learn to ride a horse, which then will lead you to learn to play polo. Also, if you want to run a marathon, start with a mile and increase it to two, then three— before you know it, your heart is trained for longer energy. These are some of the examples to achieve any specific goal you desire to achieve.

This is beyond academic credentials and attainments— how one positions oneself and conducts oneself in a public setting is key to the type of value one desires to be known for. It is to be noted that you only become valuable to people—or in return, people become valuable to you—when you're needed.

As indicated in my first book, adding value to oneself allows you to be at a level with your peers who were at one time unable to spend time with you, as most people are naturally busy with their daily activities. If you're able to add value to yourself by having credentials (or because credentials are required) or possessing things in place to merit your peers' height, you find yourself in their circles every time by default—this way, you satisfy both professional and personal assemblies at the same time.

There is a talented woman who works in a major tech company. She went in as a temporary worker, who, after a month, was taken on for a full-time job due to the value her employers saw in her. Compare her to another lady working for the same company for more than the standard minimum of three months who has still not been offered a full-time position. The first woman worked extra hard, finished her work efficiently and on time, and she continued to ask for more work to do. She took over a previous workload that took the preceding person who held that position several days to complete with so many backlogs. However, this new person finishes a full day's work in half of the time, asking for more to do. This is what we call 'adding value.' Compared to the other lady—who does her work as usual and minimal as possible, who is very conservative and closes like everyone else but expects a miracle to happen to her—do you expect she will see a different result?

Adding value to oneself could also be personal development and or adding co-curricular activities to your credentials. These could come in the form of excelling in a particular field of expertise—sport, dancing, horse riding, your presentation and communication skills and many other related concerns you have to improve.

Who knows you?

Who is clapping for you? Who is discussing you in that boardroom or privately in a positive manner? Who values your credentials and respects them in return? Who or what are you known for, and for good or bad reasons? Who knows you on a first-name basis? There may be dozens of Baake's, but when your name is mentioned will they ask, is it Baake Mensah? Even when you're known as an individual, is it based on a specific skill set that you possess? Are you recognized as a giver, value-added person, a kind or selfish person or tormentor? The answers will be based on what you have planted in people either as they perceive you or in reality.

We seem to take pride in the many people that we may have in our social media channels and claim with pride classmates that are in higher positions in society. Who have you become, and who knows and remembers you in return? These are pondering moments to some! We pose with pride with celebrities or famous people in high positions that we might have met in an event (which in itself is tremendously emotionally healing and fulfilling). We go further by posting such images all over any social media with great pride. The question is, do they know you as well, and on a first-name basis? Will they remember you when they meet you next time? As part of the pondering moment, there is much work one needs to advance to reverse the coin and become a 'go-to' person—this is the essence of adding value to oneself.

• Food for thought:

When you're endowed with a talent or specialized knowledge in a subject matter with which someone needs help, do not hesitate to assist. Be the first to offer a helping hand if you can. The knowledge could become obsolete after some time, especially after that person acquires that knowledge from somewhere else apart from you, your value diminishes, and what used to be your anchor of 'bluff' loses its effect. Add value to someone's life path, and you'll be remembered probably more than you would be for lending someone money.

Worksheet:

What type(s) of value(s) do you consider essential to add to your credentials (if any) to help promote your next steps as far as personal development, career, or work life balance is concerned?

_____

_____

_____

_____

_____

_____

_____

_____

_____

_____

_____

_____

_____

_____

_____

Worksheet

-4-

GOOD MORAL ETHICS

This is an area that sometimes becomes the Achilles heel for a lot of people. No one is exempt: I mean no one! Some people—even professional counselors who may come across as saints and perfect—sometimes fall short of this, either in the way they think or talk, the things they see, or even their secret proclivities. Yes, some may have overcome inevitable turbulence in their lives that gives them the passion and license to share their opinion and guidance. Still, the reality is this—no one is infallible. Know yourself! Before doing what you intend to do, pause a moment, and ask yourself—how will people describe you ten years down the line? If your weakness is how badly you speak, especially using foul language all the time, check yourself or get someone to be your check and be responsible by creating a money box. For example, whenever foul language comes out of your mouth, you place an agreed amount into it for charity. Let it be an amount that hurts you to release, so it serves as a deterrent to you.

The words that come out of one's mouth should be decent. I know some people who can't speak decently or with civility without using vulgar words. And when they are confronted, they go with the excuse "this is who I am" syndrome. Can you imagine such people also complaining about why their relationships aren't going well, or why they are not finding happiness where they work or how they could not maintain a good friendship? They, too, will complain—test the waters first. This is the reason when someone comes to me for any informal counseling, I listen to what I am not being told, and I pay attention to what could be hidden. I am a firm believer that what is not being said is louder than what you're telling me. It is a gift that I employ in even my consulting and corporate training, which has given me success in what I do. The reason is, people will tell you a one-sided story and, of course, their own convincing part, and if you're a careful observer, you might draw conclusions right there. I am always thinking of the other person who isn't there to defend him or herself because there are still two sides to every issue. Most of the problems we face have nothing to do with the credentials we have, but more to do with our morals and how we position ourselves.

You can have excellent credentials and accolades, but with bad etiquette, you're down. Let us not see moral ethics as living a life of perfection. Ethics are baby steps one takes to try to be a good person in his or her daily life. Morals are directly linked to how one behaves, not just in the spotlight but also behind the scenes when no one is watching. Those closest to you and who know you well put aside your credentials and relate with you regularly—just like they did in the past, way before those titles. They can even go to the extent of coming across as though they disrespect you, but nope, this is a mutual relationship that you both have, and must be maintained that way. This is separate from intentionally questionable behavior from people. There is a fine line you do not want to cross. This depends on the environment and the grouping, and calls for tact and wisdom.

Moral decency paves a unique path for you. It is ironic, though, that some people who happen to have an arrogant attitude, speak inappropriately, and have zero manners have high expectations despite the very weakness they exhibit. They desire and expect a higher standard from other people, believing life will favor them with the best career opportunities, and desire to marry from the best ethical family and attain the highest level in life. The math doesn't add up in real life. However, life is unfair sometimes, in part because, in reality, most of them do achieve their aim, and get the best while others who strive to do the right things fall short. Despite that, life is not only about money and physical acquisition, but also the mark you leave in people's lives, so that shouldn't deter you from doing it right.

• Food for thought:

Good morals reflect on you wherever you go. Just as bad habits like 'cursing' in every statement stay with you—even in professional terrain—so it is with good ethics. They transcend your generation, as your children learn to be like you and want to act in the same way you do. Practice good behavior: If you fall short, it is not too late if you're on the other end of the shore, considering no one is perfect, in that we are all on a learning curve in this life. In the end, having moral dignity can take you far. The moral strength and character of a person counts and reveals itself in moments of despair.

Worksheet:

Let me leave you with this question: what role model are you? In what field?

Also, list and discuss areas in your personal life where you consider yourself to have high morals and areas where you seem to fall short. What steps do you plan to take to turn the challenging aspects into opportunities?

_____

_____

_____

_____

_____

_____

_____

_____

_____

_____

_____

_____

_____

_____

-5-

SOCIAL ETHICS

Most people who rise to the top did not get there because of their credentials and or academic performance alone, even if they did perform well. Beyond such recognitions, there are certain critical social factors that one needs to possess to catapult them to the top.

Whether you are an executive in a Fortune 10 or small establishment, a student in Ivy-league school or a village, an aspiring employee or employer, negotiating for a big or small contract, when someone takes you out for a business lunch, do you think it's about the food? Imagine the temptation of a buffet, where every kind of food looks very appealing and drinks all calling your name. Don't fall for that irresistible temptation to sell your birthright for more significant opportunities or selling your short-term appetite for the bigger bucks. Take only a few items onto your plate, and make sure you don't pick items that are likely to spill onto your clothes. Don't lose your focus from the discussion over food. You're allowed to go for another round for fruits or food, but you need to be cautious based on the environment. A team went out to dinner to celebrate two new interns that recently joined the group. One intern went last and ordered a food item that someone else on the team ordered. The second intern, however, ordered a fillet mignon. Unfortunately, that food choice was not appropriate for such an occasion and was expensive as well. He wasn't educated on social cues. When attending a dinner with a client, or a new team or your manager, remember why you are there and remember to pay attention to social cues. Don't lose your focus on the discussion because of food—as tempting as it may be.

Having a firm handshake is essential. Your credentials reveal themselves better when you have a good handshake. Meeting a potential business partner or employer, especially for the first time, provides the opportunity to connect with that person with a good handshake and that could be the door opener. Don't squeeze, don't slide through, but grip firmly. It is a sign of confidence. It assures the other person that you know what you're about and that you can be trusted. Male to male hands shaking may be slightly different from male to female (or female to female). Be a little gentle with females but still keep it somewhat firm and quickly take your hands off. This, too, is social etiquette.

A firm handshake should go with good eye contact when you meet. Eye contact complications are cultural issues for most people. Make eye contact; make sure your eyes don't wonder. Good eye contact can make a person trust you. Bad eye contact or lack of eye contact can give the wrong impression.

On the one hand, lack of eye contact can make you seem less confident or look like a creep. Keep it professional and straightforward, especially if the person in question is the opposite sex. In some cultures, eye contact can be considered rude. Before you go into any situation, study the culture you are in and adapt accordingly.

The type of dress you wear to specific events says a lot about you and should be appropriate. We have dresses that are specific for functions and not appropriate for professional settings. You can get away with particular colors for essential functions but not for a professional environment. Be mindful of the type of event. When in doubt, keeping to traditional colors like black, blue, and light brown is safe for professional settings. The color of a tie (if you're a man) and the color of a suit or dress (if you're a woman) say much about you. Even for essential functions, investigate the culture before diving into your most expensive and favorite color. If it is a funeral, social-ethical wisdom should tell you to ask what colors are allowed at the function and dress accordingly. If it is a wedding, you cannot wear your old wedding gown (especially for women) to such a function, as this may confuse who the actual bride is. If you're unsure of what to wear, ask.

When you visit someone's house and the carpet is white and clean, and the host takes off his or her shoes, what do you do? You take off your shoes as well. You don't need a prescient to tell you this. This calls for universal wisdom. Credentials don't count here. In fact, on the contrary, your credentials will instead be questioned if you walk on that white carpet with dirt on your foot without care. A lot of things we deal with in life need common sense and social wisdom, and when applied, these will add value to you, and you will be respected even more.

Using a white carpet was just one example—as a gentleman, consider never asking a lady for her number unless she gives it to you herself. Alternatively, find a creative way to get it informally. One such creative way could be to hand yours to her and wait! Yes, I said, wait! Unless in serious business and professional settings, where you both exchange contacts for the sake of the company in question—that is allowed, or best put, socially courteous.

Avoid talking about politics, religion, or controversial topics when having business dealings. This may derail everything you desire to attain or hope to achieve in your meeting. People are sensitive to specific topics, and if not handled properly, these could turn into what are called 'diplomatic arguments,' and that might end everything you were hoping for in that meeting. This excludes when a natural opportunity comes when both of you have a common ground on a topic that could enhance your next steps. Even then, have your antenna on. However, if it is up to you, avoid it.

When you get to know someone through a link, do not snub the link that connected you in the first place. It is true that over time, your relationship with the new person or opportunity may grow, but always remember how you got into that. Be thankful and appreciative of your 'rearview mirror.'

Have fun, and do not let anyone else determine or define that for you. The reason to not let anyone else define it for you is that someone else's definition of fun may not be the same as yours. Following people blindly could lead you into many troubles in life. Stay on your course, know who you are, carry your cross—determine what works for you, and find people to enjoy it with. Don't take life too seriously, make time to 'chill'— however, also with purpose, focus, vision, persistence, and a desire to surge. 'Chill' with your eyes open—be wise.

The above are just some examples of the synopsis of living a life embedded with social wisdom.

• Food for thought:

Having social ethical wisdom is very essential in life. If added to your credentials, it will make a better version of you. Having social wisdom could cover a lot of loopholes that you may have. It increases one's perceived wisdom and confidence in society. You can learn— practice it.

Worksheet:

Which areas do you see as an opportunity to develop as far as social ethics are concerned? Remember to look into your personal life (beyond the examples in the chapter) and make that assessment and be honest about it.

_____

_____

_____

_____

_____

_____

_____

_____

_____

_____

_____

_____

_____

_____

_____

–6–

GOOD HEALTH

M erriam-Webster's dictionary defines health as the condition of being sound in body, mind, or spirit; freedom from physical disease or pain; a condition in which someone or something is thriving or doing well.

For the sake of this discussion, let's agree that there may be other parts to a person, but mainly three parts; body, mind, and soul. If so, to have true healing, we would need to consider and address all the elements, the whole, so to achieve total wellness. It is only then we can have real healing by addressing the whole being. This is similarly observed in a friend of mine's blog; thefirestone.org.

The body is an essential part of the human figure ecosystem, and one needs to take good care of it. You can determine whether you have good or bad health. To a large extent, people do. What I mean by that is that when you know smoking, for example, is terrible for you, but ignore the clear sign written on the pack, 'smoking will kill you,' and decide to smoke your lungs out, whom do you blame for any apparent repercussions? If you know excessive drinking is harmful to your health and you choose to drink your head out daily till you can't use your brain to its fullest capacity, whom do you blame? Listen, it is good once a while to enjoy social drinking, but know your limits and do not compare yourself to anyone. Someone's two glasses of wine at a social event after which he or she behaves entirely well may not be your case. You might be out of place and will start misbehaving like never before. Know yourself.

The human mind is another sensitive part that one cannot ignore. The brain controls the entire body in terms of what it can or cannot do, and where it wants to go and not to go. The mind, therefore, determines your total output, and, when not managed properly, could lead to deterioration of the entire body system. Plug into the account suitable materials, and it will produce a good result. The saying 'garbage in, garbage out' is so true. It indicates that whatever you put in is what you will harvest.

The human soul or spirit also forms the incorporeal part of man coupled with philosophy and art. While the body and mind play their role, without the soul or the spirit, one cannot arrive at their desired health destination. Not embedding the human soul within the mind and body is like having a car without fuel/electricity to propel it to move. You need all three for the entire human ecosystem to perform to its utmost best.

Good health also relates to emotional, psychological, and social life, among others. You can be physically healthy, but someone around you could be a tormentor to the extent that, whenever you think of that person, your mood gets affected negatively.

This can affect your productivity at work, in school, in your everyday life, and in everything you do. This is one of the reasons you're advised to marry your best friend rather than just a person, since you'll be spending a very long time together. Imagine having a relationship that is full of disarray—how do you go home in peace? It may be the reason some people end up confiding in excessive drinking and spending a lot of time outside their homes. I am not defending those who are lazy and who are promiscuous; they have their baggage to deal with, and they need help. However, I am referring to those segments of people who happen to be on the wrong side of life or who, just out of misguidance, made the wrong choice.

Other symptoms of ill-health which, when not identified and checked on time, could delay you mentally and physically may include overeating, and simple things such as not eating right and not exercising. Exercising, in this case, may be physical or mental.

Life isn't fair to some people, despite their every effort to be healthy, and this is no fault of theirs, they may be suffering from some physical, psychological, spiritual, and or emotional ailment that may require love and passion to heal them. The point here is having good health promotes happiness. Regardless of one's achievements, credentials, fulfillments and travels, one needs to find a good place to be healthy, if it is within their means.

Not harboring bitterness towards people can be an excellent medication for your soul. There may be people sick due to the pain they harbor in their hearts towards other people, and this can affect them emotionally and physically. Physiologically, this doesn't require pharmaceutical medication, but counseling and guidance. To clarify, you can distance yourself from toxic people to maintain your sanity, but do not hate them or wish them evil. The more you desire evil and harbor negative thoughts for them, the more you might increase the wounds of your soul. The realization that those whom you claim as enemies may be living better and with more success would aggravate your pain and sickness. Why not release yourself from such bondage and be free? Credentials or any other attainment cannot help you here unless you free your mind. The best credential, in this case, is to self-discipline. No amount of medicine can cure you unless you release these thoughts and set yourself free. Life is short guys, have some fun before it passes you by—have fun responsibly.

||||||||||||||||||||||||||||||||||||||||||||||||||||||||||||||||||||||||||||||||||||||||||||||||||||||||||||||||||||||||||||||||||||||||||||

• Food for thought:

Discussing the soul brings to mind the element of faith in connection with the spirit being. Consider entering a room and pressing a button with every hope in your gut to turn the lights on. And yes, when you pressed that switch button the lights turned on. Consider entering an airplane, not knowing who the pilots are in the cockpit to fly that plane, but hoping and believing you will get to your destination safely. That is faith too. Consider also entering a car and turning the ignition, and immediately knowing your car engine will start (unlike one of the cars I owned in my early life). That is faith. It takes faith to drop your children at school, believing you will pick them up safely after school hours. Although this has changed in most places because parents live in fear of a terrorist attack—even then, we hope and have faith that they will be safe.

The point is if we can trust natural faith (through science and technology) to use waves (things we don't see) to bring us images that enable us to watch TVs, voice recordings through radio stations, and the use of cell phones through satellite connections from space, how about divine faith too?

If you can believe in cars to perform well, the pilots at the cockpits to take us safely to our destination, then why not build your life on investigating and determining which higher power holds the four pillars of the earth and the universe (if any), or how the moon hangs in the air without falling, and even if it falls, to where? Having faith isn't particular to one religion but rather to the appreciation of a higher power in the universe.

Take a moment out of your busy life and be by yourself and ask a few personal questions about life and sincerely attempt to answer them in earnest. Try the following things; take a deep breath away from everyone, go to the beach, sit at your corridor or patio, take a walk with your dog, lie down quietly in your bed staring at the ceiling, and have a personal time with the Supreme power above. Ask questions and allow for answers over time. The answers may come or manifest in different forms—through a relative, your pet, your housemaid, colleagues, or through a dream or a deep feeling of what the truth is. There may be a higher power out there, test it.

On another note, when someone is dying of a fatal illness or from natural death or emotional distress, do you think that person is thinking of the credentials he or she possesses at that moment? People die with million dollar checks in their hands (accounts) while in their offices. That person's immediate need is healing or rehabilitation if possible—it doesn't matter whichever way you look at it. Also, when someone falls into a pit, what they seek at that very moment is to be taken out from that pit, regardless of who it is that is helping them out; they couldn't care less whether they have a degree, credentials or not. The best credential they need at that moment is a skillful person strong enough to rescue them. Let's therefore work together for the good of humanity and to attain excellent health in the three areas identified to a human being: body, mind, soul, and beyond.

Worksheet:

I shared a few nuggets on the three parts to a human being: body, mind and soul/spirit and others. Visit your innermost person to share your thoughts, experiences and what you intend to do to add value to your life in terms of achieving good health.

Also, why does it matter (after reading this chapter) to integrate healthy living (physical, emotional and social) as part of your life's happiness leading to a total healthy life?

_____

_____

_____

_____

_____

_____

_____

_____

_____

_____

_____

_____

_____

–7–

BE THANKFUL AND APPRECIATIVE

Learn to appreciate each day as it comes. Take some time off, open your window, see the light outside, enjoy the beautiful rising sun and the moon, savor, and enjoy the sight. Can you reduce, or if possible, stop, the nagging? Review the type of friends you have around you if you persist in complaining every time. Compare them to those who are positive. The negative ones (some who are crafty, because they will gossip through a medium that you least expect) always have something negative to say about the positive ones. Take a look around for a second and see. Just chill and cool it and enjoy the beautiful day, my friends.

Appreciation or gratitude is a potent source of motivation. Be grateful not only when things are good and moving in the direction you predicted. Simple things like appreciating having life today are just what you need. You are better off than someone somewhere, and as you desire to be like someone, somebody somewhere is also wishing to be like you in secret—the reason it hurts to see people committing suicide due to some difficulties or hardships that needed attention that might have been overlooked. Let's find the opportunity to make others feel comfortable in our presence. Be positive, optimistic, and believe.

Appreciation opens many other doors for you that may not have anything to do with credentials. Take, for example, a young man that I know, let's call him Yayra, who was working at a company in the U.K. Just when he joined the company, within months there came the unwelcome news—'redundancy.' The story of retrenchment was painful to take, but it was a reality, and those who joined the company the earliest also had to be laid off, and so, it was apparent Yayra would be affected.

Before the news of the redundancy saga, Yayra did some+thing unique every week that singled him out of the pack. He would write a weekly report about his daily/weekly activities and performances, detailing any challenges and opportunities he experienced. He also suggested solutions for the company to adopt. He regularly purchased postal stamps and sent the reports to the headquarters in Scotland by using his money, though he lived in London. This gentleman's name was spreading in the company with admiration, but he didn't even know about it until the day he was among the group that was supposed to be affected by the redundancy. Senior leadership called all the London employees into an office in North London, where out of respect for the employees, each one was called one by one (instead of a group message) to explain why they had to go. Almost everyone that came from that office (though it was expected) left with pain.

One by one, they went in and out. When it was Yayra's turn, he was met with about five top officials sitting on a long table. The panelist did the usual thing by appreciating him for the short time he worked there and the impact he made. However, for the company's current financial situation, they couldn't keep that large number of them, and so they offered him a nice pleasantry and other things that come with it. When they were done, the first expression and words that came out of Yayra's mouth were a huge smile and appreciation for the short-term opportunity offered to him. He expressed that he knew how difficult it must have been to make this decision. It was a necessity, he continued. Yayra ended by wishing them well in return, and as he turned to go with the usual smile and a wave, one of the influential managers yelled back, "Yayra, please stop." They asked him to wait outside for a while, and within a few minutes, they called him back into the same office. This time, they said to him they couldn't see him leave. They were impressed by his act of respect and appreciation even in such a difficult time, and also told him of the unique way that he worked by sending constant reports when he didn't have to because no one did that. They enumerated many other good things he contributed to, which were admirable. Yayra was reinstated immediately.

Being appreciative of life is essential. Specific continents like Africa are endowed with warm temperatures and beautiful weather. Some, if not most, complain of that same heat that others desire. People in other parts of the world, such as the U.S., Canada, the U.K, Russia, would do anything to trade places. No wonder when it is summertime, people take every advantage of it, knowing very well it won't last for long in the western part of the globe. I use this as an example to only show what we should be appreciative of instead of the reverse

Excuses are necessary tools for incompetence and failure. There are many people out there who with good reason could not achieve what they ought to have achieved due to circumstances not evident to the naked eye. Instead, they turn what might have been their nemesis into achieving greater heights. If people like Louis Braille, who was blind but was able to create the Braille reading for the blind, and Harriet Tubman, who was an African American slave woman able to flee tribulation and seek refuge in the north, then return to save her family, could do what they did, why not you? These and many others were able to overcome their nemesis and turn the negative into a positive, why not you, and why complain?

There is no guarantee that every time you're grateful and appreciative, opportunities will run to you, but it's the right thing to do. The act of gratitude heals and opens doors for other people to enjoy. A person's act of appreciation might be the reason a door is opened for you today, not necessarily because of how smart you are or the credentials you may have. This is something we teach our children from an early stage—three magic words; 'thank you,' 'please,' and 'sorry'! We also admonish them that 'please' is not a guarantee of getting what you want, but it is certainly polite. This is because, as you may know already, children are smart enough to sometimes abuse their opportunities. Whenever they need anything and they forget to use their 'magic words,' they immediately say, "oh sorry, can I 'PLEASE' have X, Y, Z?" We know they mean it, but we always remind them that, although it is a nice gesture, this won't necessarily get them what they wanted, although it certainly sets them apart from a moral standpoint. It's just the right thing to do.

Being polite comes with positive effects and associated benefits. You can be annoying to many but showing respect and politeness can cover a lot. Ethan, my middle son, whom I prefer to call Selassie, is one polite guy whom you cannot take for granted. He has a strong spirit, and his mind is set on what he wants, even at his tender age. He and his brothers are super caring, but he is one who can amid chaos come back to hug and thank you for everything you do for him. He is quick to say, 'I love you' and become the peacemaker. When he does something that causes him to cry, unlike some others who may ignore any affection, Selassie is the opposite. Just call him and cuddle him and he is fine. He eventually calms down and starts to seek happiness for others, not only his own. It is difficult to withhold good things from people like this; as a result, he serves as a point to cover for the rest of his siblings as well.

Besides being appreciative, honoring life through the art and habit of saying thank you to people when they do something for you sets you on a different platform. Even during times when it is expected from the person to do something like working together on a project, saying thank you for a little extra mile from the other side says a lot about you.

May it not come true, but wait until you lose what you took for granted or never appreciated. It is then you will see how valuable life has been to you. Even though this may not apply to everyone, peace, life, potential opportunities, and even short-term challenges are probably meant to toughen you and make you a better person. In essence, it all depends on how you position your mind.

• Food for thought:

In the end, be genuine about what you say, and mean it! Someone can answer always with 'thank you,' 'sorry,' and 'please' to show politeness, but may not mean it in his or her heart. This is like someone kneeling before you, but in their heart boastful and standing. Likewise, someone can be standing on you but polite within. It is all about perspective and approach. Being appreciative and polite is not a license for others to treat you with disrespect. It is also not a sign of intimidation. Do not confuse it. Be firm, bold, assertive, confident, but in all, learn the habit of affability.

You can chase and have all the credentials you can get, the fame that comes with it, and the knowledge, but without appreciation of what you have, life to you will be shallow and hollow. Take some time off from your busy life and treat yourself well. I mean, open that window and enjoy the breeze that comes through it. See the beauty of the heat and the cold, snow and wind, or take a walk on the beach and enjoy nature's beauty and offerings. Friends, find your happiness in life and appreciate it—do that now! Credentials are essential, but they won't do it for you entirely.

Though you may not be where you want to be as far as your life's goal is concerned, be grateful regardless for how far you are from where you came from.

Worksheet:

Do you think being appreciative and being thankful is part of a healthy life living? Explain.

_____

_____

_____

_____

_____

_____

_____

_____

_____

_____

_____

_____

_____

_____

_____

_____

_____

_____

– 8 –

SURROUND AND BE SURROUNDED BY GOOD FRIENDS AND LOVED ONES

Before you jump into a quick conclusion that good friends and loving family surround you, wait until you fall into a problem and see the distance they may give you. During stressful times, you can determine who truly loves you. Test the waters first—is everything going so well that you were blinded and drew an inaccurate conclusion? Sometimes, it is good to verify the truth. If, however, all is going in the right direction around you, you are lucky and blessed. Cherish those who love, care, and fall in such a unique category and always return a similar favor.

Otherwise, take a moment to look around and review the type of people within the mass of your circle of friends and loved ones—I don't necessarily mean those whom you see every day by default by the nature of your work or environment alone. There are some special people whose presence provides fulfillment with a great sense of joy. Regardless of status, you enjoy each other. This could be because you have something that they cherish, which is usually reciprocal.

There are three possible types of people that may surround you, and the reverse may be true:

- Those who help you
- Those who hurt you
- Those that don't care

Segment your loved ones into these three categories, and you'll start making serious decisions. Some come across as helping you, but in reality, are hurting your dreams. In retrospect, are you only at the receiving end? What role do you play in the life of your loved ones, especially concerning the above three scenarios?

The decision to be positive or negative, to succeed or to fail, to upgrade yourself or not, to learn a trade or profession, to have the right attitude or not, depends on the type of people you surround yourself with.

Oh, please, do not be fooled by the arsenal of 'friends' and 'loved ones' you may have when you're on top of life's ladder, at the height and pinnacle of your career and with a lot of money and many opportunities. Interrogate such friends and loved ones and make sure they are, genuinely, who they say they are. If such positions are no more in existence, there, you'll see how many lean friends you'll have. Your Christmas presents will shrink to the bare minimum. I don't expect to be burned for being wrong on this—yes, who knows? I might be, and I know most, if not some of such acquaintances may be authentic and remain loyal regardless of where you land in life, but my point here is that not all those who surround you may be real—some have an agenda. Cross-examine, investigate, test, and be sure you will always land in safe hands when falling from the sky without a parachute. In all honesty, do a little research on famous people who once attained high positions that naturally attracted lots of loved ones and supporters—when they suddenly fell from their height, how many diehards stayed by their sides? The truth here is, only a few remain loyal. Friendship is a two-way road. Meaning, you too should remain who you are to your buddies. These types of assessments may not be written in any average academic or credential manual because hard truths are rare to come by.

"Surround yourself with people that push you to do better. No drama or negativity. Just higher motivation. Good times and positive energy. No jealousy or hate. Simply bringing out the best in each other".

- Warren Buffett -

I give 100% credit to New Look Organization for this message that went viral with a few additions: "There is a story about a former undersecretary of defense who was invited to give a speech at a large conference. He was standing on the stage with a cup of coffee in a Styrofoam cup with his prepared PowerPoint presentation behind him. He took a sip of his coffee and smiled, and he looked down at the coffee, and then he went off-script and he said, you know last year I spoke at this exact same conference. Last year, I was still the undersecretary and they flew me here business class. And when I arrived at the airport, there was somebody waiting to take me to the hotel that was already checked in for me, so they just took me up to my room. The next morning, I came downstairs and there was someone waiting in the lobby to greet me, and they drove me to this same venue. They took me through the back entrance and took me into the green room and handed me a cup of coffee in a beautiful ceramic cup. He then said, I am no longer the undersecretary. I flew here coach. I took a taxi to my hotel and checked myself in. When I came down the lobby this morning, I took another taxi to this venue. I came in the front door and found my way backstage and when I asked someone do you have any coffee, he pointed to the coffee machine in the corner and I poured myself a cup of coffee into this here Styrofoam cup (as he raised the cup in his hands). He said, the lesson is the ceramic cup was never meant for him (as a person), it was meant for the position he held. He went on to say, I deserve a Styrofoam cup.

Remember this, as you gain fame, as you gain fortune, as you gain position and seniority, people will treat you better. They will hold doors open for you. They will get you a cup of tea and coffee without you even asking. They will call you sir and ma'am and they will give you stuff. None of that stuff is meant for you (as a person), that stuff is meant for the position you hold. It is meant for the level that you have achieved or whatever you want to call it, but you will always deserve a Styrofoam cup. Remember the lesson of humility and gratitude. You can accept all the free stuff. You can also accept all the perks, absolutely you can enjoy them (provided they are legal and does not conform to any conflict of interest), but just be grateful for them and know that they're not for you, they're for your position. This goes to remind us that, none of us deserve the perks that we get, we all deserve a Styrofoam cup." Very revealing, isn't it?

The habit of quieting the noise around you sometimes, so as to enable you listen to the true feelings about people around you, is essential—not only people who are physically close to you alone but also those who are distant physically, emotionally, in your mind and your spirit. Ask yourself, are they around me, or am I around them because of wealth, opportunities, or for a reason other than what you will gain from each other? It is not a bad thing to be surrounded for such reasons, but you need to know, so that you're not disappointed when the time comes. Such people vanish immediately when the expected opportunity ceases to exist. Ironically, it gets sometimes lonely when you're at the pinnacle of success because, though there are many people around you, you don't seem to have true happiness and the right people to share your issues with. Though you have people around you, deep inside, you can often feel alone. This is the main reason making rational choices is more beneficial than emotional ones. Emotions affect your actions, perceptions, and behavior. Remove the blindfold to see clearly.

"Watch the raccoons in your life—raccoons are the distractions that you need to be aware of, they are the shining objects. Don't let distractions keep you away from your destiny because there are many distractions and noises out there. One of the ways to catch a raccoon is to distract it by showing it a shiny object."

- Synergy and Commonality, The Key to Success -

Sometimes you feel you have a connection with a group, but trust me, only time will tell before you know its actual purpose—linked to the job, the environment, the prospects they desire from you. When those things are gone, and they are no more, you cease to exist, at least in their minds. Do not fool yourself. Build positive and forward-looking relationships. Test those relationships and see the reaction. Sometimes people are together and doing okay until something happens, and immediately their true nature reveals itself. It may be too late at the time, so the need to prune rough-edges along the journey before the destination is crucial.

Some people are just too toxic to hang around with. They are always negative: they won't praise you when you're achieving anything good—they always find a good reason why your achievement is basic and how others are doing the same. They will undermine every step you desire to pursue because until they are the ones in the helm of affairs, whatever you do is useless. Why hang too long with such people? You can be subtlety wise around them and stay friends but not too close as far as your mind and ideas are concerned. Also, consider not disowning people because of their divergent ideas. Determine the difference between someone who is challenging your thoughts to become a better person and someone who is obviously against any positive step you decide to engage in and does not have alternatives for you. Spend time with quality people who will add value to you.

If you surround yourself with three negative people (be it family or friends), soon you'll be the fourth. Note that ships don't sink because of the water that surrounds them, or the water they travel on. They sink mainly because of the water that enters them, so avoid negative thoughts and the ship sinkers. Some people in your life may be detrimental to your progress— in part, no matter what you do or achieve, they will always undercut it. Why waste your little time on earth with such people? Love them from a distance—they are bottlenecks.

The Internet reflects what you're seeking. Type anything you want, and you'll find the result. Therefore, be careful about what you're looking for. It can reveal the good, bad, and ugly. If you want to know only negative things about the most gifted person on earth, the Internet will help you find it, so use it positively—while you seek to surround yourself with great people, also aspire to be great so others can rely on you, in a two-way process. Humans are like wet rags. If you genuinely want to know what it contains, give it a little squeeze, and you'll see what it reveals. The question here is, does the person in question want to remain negative or are they aspiring to be great? Help each other reach the heights of life.

What kind of person are you to others? While you wish to be surrounded by good people, others are also evaluating to see if you're a good fit for them. Some people take advantage of this situation to segregate others, but avoid such behavior and find a true fit based on the better person version of you that you aspire to be. It is like a woman who has written a long list of things she wants to have and see in a man before she considers marrying him. What she has forgotten is that, the specific man that meets those qualifications may also have a long list and will expect a particular type of person due to the value he has in himself. Iron sharpens iron. You need to be prepared for what you seek to have and be ready to fit the cover of the bottle you seek.

• Food for thought:

People aren't naturally bad, but they can have bad intentions. Someone who once was an angel to you could turn on you within seconds. They produce negative energy and influence probably due to many factors—the current life stage they are in, their unhappiness with your progress, their disdain for you because you're overtaking where they think you ought to be in life, or just that they may be experiencing a bad relationship, or they made a new friend who is influencing them. As a result of any of the above and even beyond, they may be smearing back at you. Those with whom you spend a lot of time reveal who you are. Don't judge them, but advise yourself on how to live around them. You can be with them physically but not emotionally or mentally if you have to. Best of all, avoid cuddling with such people—it's all about timing and use of your gut feelings.

If not appropriately managed, such people could damage your reputation, credibility, opportunities, and credentials, and you'll be perceived in the wrong light. If there is a way you can help them through third-party counseling, please do, but don't play in the pit of the snake. Simply put, there comes a time in your life when you need to assess those whom you are surrounded with.

Worksheet:

Share a list of five to ten good friends and loved ones you have in your circle who would stand with you through thick and thin. Why do you think they will stick with you, regardless of your life's outcome?

_____

_____

_____

_____

_____

_____

What relations do you need to cut off and which ones do you need to amend or improve?

_____

_____

_____

_____

_____

_____

_____

-9-

EMBRACING THE POWER OF DIVERSITY

*"If you look at each spoke of the wheel independently,
it appears to be leading in a different direction from all the
others. But that is only because each is starting
from a different direction point, and to reach the same
endpoint, it has to head in the unique direction that is
expected to take it to the "hub" of truth, just as each of us
travels a different path to reach the same ultimate truth."*

- Pat McKelvey -

Being able to live and work with people from diverse backgrounds has become a necessary skill. No matter how smart one is, how generous one can be, and how great one becomes, one cannot succeed in any endeavor if they can't coexist with other people. I usually use the human body as a metaphorical analogy to describe such situations. The body has many parts, but it is one person. The hands play their role in what it is created to perform, and must do their best to contribute to the body ecosystem's perfect performance. The head/brain is meant to think; imagine using it to walk. Imagine expecting the legs to think when they are naturally intended to walk. Misplacing priorities and not allowing everyone to perform their duties the way they are made or trained to perform them eliminates the power of synergy. In essence, true value diminishes, leading to decreased efficiency and effectiveness.

Some people are born with particular disabilities who end up doing extraordinary things through adaptation; they are different and unique and must be respected for what they can do. It's a shame some of us who are endowed with everything complain and can't coexist with each other when such disabled people instead perform their duties with such perfection— using their mouth to paint, for example.

I have come to understand that most people who frown on others, especially from other cultures, may be people who have not traveled outside their territory to be exposed to the realities of life. They seem confined in their bubble and think the world is only what they know. Some also may not have had the opportunity to work in a big firm that has a presence all over the globe, for which one is forced to work with everyone regardless of race, ethnicity, skin tone, gender, belief, social orientation, or their last names.

We are too busy fighting each other and finding differences we have that we don't spend enough time to love one another, care for one another, accept one another, or appreciate the beauty of diverse cultures and what they bring. If a car has only one tire rolling, where will you sit? It takes the various parts of that car to move so that you arrive at your destination. The same should be considered for human beings who are expected to act in a certain way when working together.

"The forces that unite us are intrinsic and greater than the superimposed influences that keep us apart."

- Dr. Kwame Nkrumah -

One should know that everyone is an immigrant in one way or another. It doesn't take too long to determine this. Just review your family history, and you'll see your origination. We have all migrated one way or another from somewhere to a place at a point in time, and we settle where we think it is most safe. Some don't even have to review any lineage, like my children. They know where their parents came from initially and see the need to embrace everyone as one. The only difference with various migrants is the fact that some came earlier, and others arrived later. Almost every country or continent was founded by people who decided to settle there for so many reasons, including safety, economic reasons, religious freedom, greener pastures, the beauty of a place, landscape, the land's potential, and the like. The fact that some others arrived first should not create segregation amongst people, but rather they should be able to live together in peace. I am passionate about equality and defending the cause for the deprived and destitute, not to mention social advocacy for human rights—at least the ones I believe in. One may not agree or believe in all facets of the human rights movement, and I may not find it in all, but there are fundamental areas one cannot ignore.

Specific languages like English have only become the dominant lingua franca in the world arguably and mainly because of the wealth their speakers possess and their superpower dominance to a certain degree. If tomorrow the Chinese take over the world through their economic power, everyone will want to speak Chinese in addition to their native dialect. And the same will occur with African languages, Dutch, or Latin, when they take over one day. In all these, it is clear that speaking one language going forward isn't enough. People feel respected and welcome when they see your effort in trying to speak their dialect or language, even if your speech is not perfect. The point here is to embrace diversity in language as well.

There is a modernized form of discrimination these days in which certain people accept you for who you are, but in their hearts and minds feel they are only doing you a favor by being your friend. How can this be? To a large extent, once this is not hypocritical but a genuine effort to get to know you, it must be applauded as a step towards civility and normalization of life. Eventually, though, if it has to be done, then it must be done well. Why is this difficult, anyway? Detach yourself from people who, for a certain reason, discriminate against others—in terms of the color of their skin, their race, religious beliefs, et cetera, et cetera! Imagine falling sick at a spot where you are only surrounded by people you don't like or relate with—let's see who will rush to you and call for help. Let's not make this negative. What would happen if, when the next door in your life opens, you only see those whom you despise sitting to make a decision and recommendation about your significant next step for a brighter future? Those who fall short of this, remember, no one is perfect; give yourself another chance to make it right. Sometimes, through no fault of your own, you might be ill-informed or refuse to educate yourself regarding the facts about other cultures and lifestyles apart from what you know and are comfortable with. You need help with patience and love.

"I don't like that man. I must get to know him better."

- Abraham Lincoln -

Once again, learn to embrace unity through diversity and respect each other's viewpoints. It is wise and best to bring together people from every field of expertise in order to succeed. Diversity (age, ideas and culture) provides you or the company the benefit of having different experiences and perspectives—which leads to delivering a quality product or service. As mentioned earlier, regarding the roles played by the human body system, every individual part has been placed on you to fulfill a purpose within the ecosystem of the human body. Every component is designed and put in its specific position to perform a duty. The eye cannot tell the ear, "I don't need you." How would you hear then? The ear cannot say to the eye, "I don't need you." How would you see without it?

Yes, some are gifted to see through feelings, but that is a particular case. If the leg decides to be the head and the head goes on strike and becomes the stomach, how effectively will you survive to perform your daily chores? In the same way, the human race exists for a reason. The Black, White, Irish, African, American, Asian, Greek, Italian, and many others are created for a purpose. Unfortunately, we spend too much time counting the differences we have, presuming that one is better than other, instead of directing our focus to what binds us together. Even in a business sense, individual establishments may take a steep hill to succeed if they do not include the local culture as part of their leadership team. Regardless of your credentials, market knowledge, and network, the locals quickly assess these things to determine their support for you or not. Basic wisdom must be applied. What fascinates me is when people act as though they contributed to how they were created. For example, if you are forty years old, where was your existence forty-two years ago? Regardless, if you descend from a rich or low-income family, born in a manger or the queen's palace, with a silver spoon or a wooden fork, we all need to be humble and appreciate who we are and respect each other's cultures and the beauty of the diversity we have.

Speaking of diversity, usually the first thing that comes to mind is the skin tone and ethnicity. What about ideas? What about diversity in the type of foods we like? What about the different sports we support? Have you thought of the different desires and tastes we have too? What about the type of spouses we prefer and the colleges we intend to attend? Can we leave out diverse aspirations, ambitions, circles of friends, and much more we cannot mention here as part of the diversity that I am referring to? Yes, of course, color and race also form part of it, but too much attention has been given to these unfairly. It is in diversity that the best ideas pop up. You may all be white females on a round table deliberating on critical development in a particular field. Still, you will receive various opinions about the solution you want—that too is diversity. You may play on an all-black soccer team with different positions—that also is a diversity of roles. You may work on a unique project with people of a combination of all—due to everyone's experiences, the thought process will differ until you arrive at the best solution—that too is diversity.

• Food for thought:

Consider this, as explained by one of the poems from my senior brother Menson Richard featured in my first book: "When racism is pointed at a particular group of people in society, they denounced racism, insisting that all men are created equal, but comes back home and practices tribalism. It's like the tortoise telling you, there's no need to run but lend him horses' legs and see. The horse may wait to be ridden but tortoise would not wait even to be ridden. With no one riding it, the same tortoise would flee. In that same vein, the poor claim the rich are a pain but let a little money come their way and you would see the true display of vanity." So it is with embracing diversity.

Let's oppose those who believe that life's natural way is to see people with similar background, color, or ethnicity as necessarily living together—this is not natural or always true. Diversity is beyond ideas, ethnicity, social orientation, or origin—it's mainly about acceptance. Let's embrace!

Worksheet:

List five areas where you fall short of wholly embracing diversity, and list five other areas you intend to improve your mindset and perspective to become a better individual.

_____

_____

_____

_____

_____

_____

_____

_____

_____

_____

_____

_____

_____

_____

_____

_____

-10-

CULTURAL BALANCE AND AWARENESS

I recall how we defined 'culture' when we were young and in early school. It was crucial to get the meaning stuck in your brain, or else you were in trouble—*Culture is the way and life of people in a particular geography.* Assuming this is true, then what is actually defined as the way of life of people in a specific location? One must adapt to a way of life and try to emulate it in order to fit in, and for those who desire to engage in business activities in that geography, to permeate successfully one has to relate. It is about understanding people's motives, sense of humor, what makes them tick and what doesn't. One must also know what their priority is and how to meet them at a convenient point to have a fruitful relationship.

Understanding different cultures helps one surge in life. Now, culture has transcended beyond just a geographical area and has become a generational stage where most people, regardless of their location, think alike, behave the same, and have similar expectations and aspirations. The current society we live in has also become super judgmental and critical of everything—this, too, is a culture that must be embraced. Other perspectives are discussed below. This is why marketing is targeted and tailored not only for a specific location but now towards the mindset and based on individual lifestyle regardless of location on the globe—thanks in part to the internet.

While the above is true, typical consideration of indigenous culture must also be taken into account. Consider, for example: exchanging business cards is not just a style but comes with respect and culturally accepted norms. When an Asian person presents you with a business card, the first thing you do is receive it with two hands, turn it, and read the credentials on it. Then, look back at them and acknowledge it with a nod of admiration. Do not place that card in your wallet and sit on it as is usually done in the western part of the world. That is an insult. Regardless of your credentials, you can lose your business contract as a result.

In Africa, during the funerals of young people, the colors black or red are the dress code. Wearing white during such an event indicates your happiness for the event. In reverse, when an older person dies, white is the recommended color, to celebrate a life well-lived. Interesting contrast, but so it is. It is therefore suggested to study each culture you're in to dress appropriately to a specific event.

In terms of cultural differences, no one chooses their culture at birth. One can decide to change their culture upon becoming an adult, but otherwise you are born into it and should be proud of your origin—who you are and where you come from. Taking into consideration cultural differences in life and business is crucial to success, ignoring them is a disaster.

It is a sad situation to be placed in a prejudged situation before you're allowed or forced to prove yourself because of your cultural origin, your looks, how you speak, sound, how you dress, or even the color of your skin, et cetera—it becomes a steep hill. The onus is on you to not look down on yourself but rather turn the perceived negative attitude into something positive. Prejudgment of someone is a disease because until you get close to that person, you may not understand why they behave in a certain way. For example, if you see someone wearing a business suit to a farm, you may begin to laugh at him or her, but that may be the last attire available to them. Give people the benefit of the doubt and get close to understanding them first.

While it may seem as though this aspect of the cultural discussion is limited to persons, we also have organizational culture and ways of doing things. If an organization decides the color green is their stop sign and not red, it is only going to be understood and practiced in that organization and nowhere else—but it must be accepted and adhered to. A reputable company I know, for example, has an interesting culture for their night shift workers, where they call their long midnight break 'lunch,' which may sound odd, but that's what they have adopted, and it works for them. Because the lower staff works mostly on a shift basis, with daily rotations, they refer to the last day of anyone's work week as their Friday, depending on the individual's shift. However, that particular day might not be Friday in itself. The point here is, this is their culture, and it works for them. And so, it is with other institutions.

In contrast, consider the traffic light as a universal cultural language. Regardless of what each color means in any culture, the traffic signal lights mean the same everywhere. Though the color red may mean one thing in China, and the same red may mean the opposite in another culture, however, on a traffic light, red only means one thing—STOP! The same goes for the yellow and the green indicators on the traffic light system. One does not need to speak or understand a particular language to drive in another country as far as traffic light indication is concerned. Of course, the road signs may be written in the local language, but when it comes to the command of the traffic light system and its signals, it is a universal language. Can you imagine the world having one understanding and one language? What peace might await us?

On business terrain, one cannot deny how culture affects the way business is done—You must embrace the notion of understanding and respecting local sensitivities if you desire to succeed. Consider the automaker Chevrolet, whose brand "Nova" sold poorly and failed in Spanish-speaking countries in its early years of production just because its name translates as "doesn't go" or "can't go" in Spanish. The Nova might have been one of the fastest cars made at the time, but because the name contradicted what it was made to do, it failed. Names count in different cultures and must be watched.

When Procter & Gamble first released its laundry detergent Cheer to Japan, according to research, it was marketed as an all-temperature detergent, something that was very popular in the United States at the time. What the brand failed to take into account was that the Japanese typically preferred washing their clothes in cold water or lukewarm bathwater; therefore, the all-temperature distinction meant little to them. Later, when the country's cultural norms were factored and appropriately marketed, its new detergent, Ariel, emphasized how well the product worked in cold water. As a result, Ariel was accepted and was successful, eventually claiming the number three market position at the time.

The use of first names in certain cultures is considered rude, while it is hailed in others. In the western part of the globe, seldomly do you call someone by their last name, titles, or credentials, but instead speak mainly on a first-name basis, unless in formal settings. In Africa, you dare not speak to someone who has spent numerous years acquiring their accolades without addressing them properly or giving the appropriate salutations; this is mostly regarded as offensive. Hugging in certain cultures is welcomed and seen as standard, while it is frowned upon in others. Shaking hands is acceptable in one but not in another. We live in a diverse world, and even though we cannot satisfy every culture and everyone, we must make an effort to be seen trying if we want to live in peace and harmony.

As illustrated in my first book, showing the sole of your shoes or feet in Arab countries is regarded as an insult in that culture. It was recorded that former U.S. Congressman Bill Richardson learned that lesson the hard way on a delicate diplomatic mission to Iraq in 1995 under Bill Clinton's presidency. Richardson crossed his leg while talking to Saddam Hussein at the time. He was dismayed initially, not knowing why Saddam left the room amidst intense discussions and negotiations. However, it was later revealed that, that particular mistake might have cost U.S. taxpayers a lot, as the talk was not as fruitful as it was meant to be. The key takeaway is for them to have studied the Iraqi culture before visiting.

• Food for thought:

Cultural balance and awareness are directly involved in embracing diversity. Accepting other people's cultures and genuinely desiring to know more about them is healing and creates a natural sign of peace. Test it!

Worksheet:

Share your experience in areas you have fallen short of accepting people in your domain.

_____

_____

_____

_____

_____

_____

_____

Also, share times when you have experienced rejection. What was the reason?

_____

_____

_____

_____

_____

_____

_____

–11–

HAVING BROAD-KNOWLEDGE AND EXPOSURE

gnorance is like a disease, and until cured of it, you will continue to live in your bubble, thinking the world revolves around you—that your mothers' dish, for example, is the best on earth. On a lighter note, however, my late mother's rice and beans dish, was an exception nevertheless! In essence, she was just the best at it. Of course, having tasted and tried many others, I was able to convince my wife, who is a great cook herself, to admit this, even though she never had the opportunity to taste my mother's meals before she passed away in blessed memory—only based on testimonials! But the main point is that escaping from narrow-mindedness will serve you better.

Ignorance keeps you in a small world of your own until you decide to avail your mind to see things differently. The least you can do is read good educational books, get close to someone who knows better than you, attend open lectures on issues of international affairs—just to mention a few. The gap between ignorance and knowledge is both vast and short at the same time; If you don't know anything about a particular subject matter, you become fascinated when you see it for the first time. For example, if you're a novice in the usage of a 'pivot table' in an excel spreadsheet to analyze big data, seeing someone navigating through it makes you nervous, and you may ask yourself, "When will I also know and master this?" At that time, the gap may seem broad and far. However, when you learn to master the use of that same tool, all of a sudden it becomes a way of life and easy to use. Looking back, the distance between what you didn't know and now know becomes so short in your sight—this is the elimination of ignorance.

Also, only when someone travels or is exposed to things outside of where they originally live will their mindset begin to change. I know a segment of people in particular who, although successful in their fields of work, are very limited in their understanding of other people's cultures, especially when such people come from other parts of the world other than what they are used to. Anytime they approach such people, they always presume they are doing them a favor as said earlier—by being their friend, talking to them, calling them on the phone, working with them, considering them as playmates, and walking with them. This is a mistake.

I have the opportunity to guest lecture at many schools and tertiary institutions, including that of Metropolitan State University in Colorado, USA, where I teach about the ethics of journalism in Africa. In my first few slides, before delving into the nitty-gritty of the main topic, I share a few slides depicting how Africa is perceived and what indeed it stands for. I show, for example, photos of dilapidated houses and ask if this is Africa, and the students jump in affirmation. Then I also show beautiful mansions with golden touches and swimming pools on the next slide and ask where that could be? The apparent answers, on average, have no space for Africa. And I tell them that this too is Africa. I go on to say, "I have a house in Africa, do you think I built and live in a hut there?" Then they all raise their eyes and say no way—and so, I tell them, while I am not defending the hardships on specific continents, not all that are shown on TV screens are true. They need to travel themselves and experience different locations to have first-hand information before they judge or jump to a conclusion—especially as they study journalism. This is one of my favorite lectures, where I give back and have excellent relationships with faculty. Ignorance is a disease and can only be cured through education, reading, experience, and learning.

I was at Heathrow airport in London sometime flying back to the United States. I was on my computer working while waiting to board my next flight when I eavesdropped on a conversation right behind me between an American White man and an African American man. The White man was telling this African American man that he was worried about people, especially in America, who are narrow-minded and who haven't traveled to see the realities of the world. He wanted them to travel outside of the United States to have broad knowledge because he believed their mindset would change when they did. He also said he wasn't referring to them traveling to Canada and Mexico, but to places like Ghana and other African and developing regions of which they might have a negative perception. He was returning from Ghana (I think he has a business there), and he was overwhelmed by the welcome accorded him—the unique culture, food, knowledge, experience, and lifestyle which is opposite to what most expect.

The conversation caught my attention because this has been my message to many on the other side for years, and of course, the mention of Ghana (my native country) made it all real to me. I jumped into the conversation smoothly, and we learned a good lesson from one another. It was surreal. I had this same conversation with a high-ranking staffer at Capitol Hill during one of my United Nations advocacy duties. This woman shared her amazement at what she experienced in Ghana when she learned I was a native—the food, the people, the art, music, and literature was unbelievable, she said. Let me use this opportunity to speak for other countries that might be looked down upon—I urge all to travel and visit new places because your first-hand knowledge is your power. Life may not be the same as it is here in the United States or other advanced countries, but it is also not the way it is described.

My wife, who used to work for one of the biggest tech companies with global worldwide operations, as part of our general information-sharing conversations, shared a non-confidential experience she had in the office during one of their meetings. The gist was that one of their staff in a developing country passed away because this staff member (who was in an Asian country) did not follow basic instructions, and when he fell backward, they had to use a motorbike to rush him quickly to the hospital. In this hospital, the doctor, instead of conducting a general scan on his head to determine the cause, just took what the staff told him, believing he had suffered just a small fall. The doctor only prescribed pain medications and sent him home. Later that night, the staff member died.

The leadership back in the United States fumed about this case and asked a fundamental question; why didn't they use an ambulance? This conversation was going on until my wife couldn't take it any longer and, according to her, educated them on how some other parts of the world work. She indicated that in some regions, though there is an ambulance, you use the most immediate available means of transport to get to the hospital. And so, what they did by using a motorbike to transport him, wasn't wrong, except, the doctor should have gone beyond what the patient had mentioned to save his life. Upon hearing this, their jaws dropped in surprise. Not every part of a developing country experiences this, as it was a unique circumstance.

The point above showed how ignorant the leadership was; despite the number of years they might have been working, they were limited to the western world's standards—while making decisions affecting every part of the globe. They might be technically competent, well-educated, and good at what they do, but they weren't exposed broadly to the realities of how things work in other parts of the world. And this is a global company. This is the reason some of us have taken it upon ourselves to jump into the wagon to provide training beyond just the technical aspects, teaching soft skills that money cannot buy to such industry leaders to add value to their knowhow with strategies that go with it. Knowledge is power and can help one become a better leader.

Some executives who find themselves in a global institution or want to have a footprint in other countries are making serious decisions on end roads in those continents; however, they have no clue how business dynamics operate there. Investing in hiring or consulting with the right person(s) who understands the mindsets and how business is done there will save money, time, and energy, and eliminate waste and other related financial loss when done the first time correctly.

|||||||||||||||||||||||||||||||||||||||||||||||||||||||||||||||||||||||||||||||||||||||||||||||||||||||||||||||||||||||||||||||||||||||||||

• Food for thought:

Most times, the difference between ignorance and wisdom is lack of knowledge and exposure. Living your life entirely on perception is a recipe for disaster—so do not judge anything by its cover alone. Go more in-depth, be inquisitive, and conduct relevant research that covers 360 degrees of the story about what you are seeking to know—you'll find the truth.

Worksheet:

Mention some cases in which you have given a wrong judgement and what it led to.

_____

_____

_____

_____

_____

_____

_____

In what ways do you often acquire new knowledge?

_____

_____

_____

_____

_____

_____

_____

-12-

MINDSET AND KNOWLEDGE

Almost everything we do in life has our mindset as a substantial contributing element. How we look at ourselves, how we look at others, how others look at us, and most importantly, how we indeed are, become the essential tools for success in life. Our mind controls almost everything we do and what we accept to be possible. Our lives are geared more towards perception than reality, so it is incumbent on us before we make up our mind or make any decision to think it through twice before acting on it.

Many people are in psychological, social, and economic bondage but refusing its existence. If you see yourself as inferior because of how you look or sound, there is little you can do in life. On the other hand, if you're bold and confident (not cocky) about your personality (who you are), reminding yourself that you did not create yourself but that your destiny is in your hands, then the sky will be the beginning point of your life's journey. This is just one example to follow.

I know of people who are stuck in the way they think about issues simply because of how they have been brought up. They will not take a little bit of time to investigate for themselves why people act in a certain way but instead judge them, mostly negatively. Using history as an example, have you made time to interrogate history regarding who the true Jews are, those regarded the original ones versus those who adopted its practices? What about when it was said Christopher Columbus found America? Is that all the story, and is it true that no single soul was living on the land apart from the Native Americans before he got to land? Have you researched civilization and where it indeed came from, and who were the ancient leaders and who migrated from place to place? What about the Egyptian rulers and the pyramids—which culture and race were they? Check out their original noses and not the reinvented ones and determine for yourself. Let's go on! Why the name Jamaica, in the Caribbean?

It is believed slaves were left on the shores in the Caribbean who couldn't be brought to America because it was believed they were causing problems among the slaves on the ship. Did the name (Jamaica) come from the Ghanaian' Twi' dialect words *Jama ya ka*, meaning *it looks like we are left behind*? What about many mighty women warriors that existed in the past from all races—where are their names in the history books? Men were meant to be the heroes and were regarded as the head, and so the brevity of these women, their contributions, and their history have been buried, and no one hears about them. So, it is not surprising that they are nowhere to be found. Refusing to know the truth or to dig into what you're told is not an excuse for the nonexistence of the fact. This is one of the reasons I love the quote from Ronald Reagan, "Trust but verify." I brought some of the above examples to provoke your mind, to possibly give you a thought and lay the foundation for you to start thinking beyond what you're told, or what you think you know. It's all about mindset based on what you read and know.

If you think someone always needs to lead you for you to succeed, so will your mindset be positioned. Some people can't think for themselves even if they are left alone in a hole—someone needs to come and decide for them what to do, and in fact sometimes remind them that they are in a mess. Seeking a second opinion or collaboration is not the same as waiting for someone to always decide for you. I always seek ideas from my wife and my children on most things, including writing this book. I seek their thoughts and their unique angles from which they see a particular subject, as well as interviewing friends and business partners. I also do this indirectly, through observation and experience. However, in some unique circumstances, you need to respect your personal opinion and stick with it if it is good. Listen to that quiet message swimming through your veins and honor it. You don't need someone to tell you to run away from an oncoming truck that could hit you. In metaphorical terms, that is how a lot of people act in life. Mindset is everything.

A healthy mindset is necessary to sustain a firm will, persistence, resilience, determination, and focus. If you decide to do anything and put your mind to it, you can do it. I hated mathematics and anything that had to do with calculating when I was young, and so I did everything within my power to avoid it, but not for long. Guess what? Everywhere I went, calculations followed me. I needed mathematics to move ahead on every stage in my career. Even when I was pursuing my M.B.A., Financial and Managerial Mathematics were at my doorstep. Yes, I got my A's and B's, but never liked it the way others liked it and gloated over their grades. Look at me now. I am a lean Six Sigma Black Belt, using a lot of statistical analysis to solve institutional problems. Most of my previous life is now dominated by using a combination of calculations to arrive at a result. I had to put my mind to it and believe in myself that I could do it, and I did. It's all about mindset.

Whatever you put your mind to, you can achieve. It is the mind that is used for everything. If you feed your mind with poison, you'll die. If you feed it with nutrients, it will nourish you. I have always had a sharp and focused mind ever since I was a child. My philosophy has always been not to allow anything to come between me and the fulfillment of my aim. Most of the dreams I had and wanted to achieve are being achieved one after the other with one step at a time, along with focus, determination, poise, perseverance, and persistence— though some achievements may be coming late, like becoming this accidental author. However, it all starts from the mind first. If you breed the mind and tell yourself that you cannot attain that height, trust me, you won't achieve it. Your dreams of failure will come to pass. This is mainly because you have already infused defeat into your body system. If, however, you reverse that thought by regrouping your mind and telling yourself, "If someone else can do it, I can too," there you go! A new birth of hope emerges in your spirit. Otherwise, the negative signals are sent to your entire body, affecting what you do, how you act, how you receive information, and your total demeanor in whatever you find yourself doing, thereby stealing your natural blessings. You will have little or no fulfillment. However, if you do the opposite, by affirming to yourself, "It is well. I can make it. There is nothing impossible under the sun; all I need is to focus, and that it is easy," there you go! The signals enhance your body; it is empowered and energized for action. It is like a boxer who had been training for a fight for a long time and is ready to blow someone out of the boxing ring. Put it this way: There are no boundaries you cannot overcome or barriers you cannot jump over. It's all about mindset.

• Food for thought:

Credentials are good—in fairness, I have quite a few of them—but they aren't the only tool that has pushed me forward. They did open the doors for me, but adding a healthy mindset, street knowledge, training, and basic social etiquette to my credentials has sustained me.

Worksheet:

Whether you succeed or fail depends on what you tell or feed your mind—it's all about the mindset. Share the extent to which you agree or disagree with the statement and what you'll be doing differently in a positive way to add value to yourself.

_____

_____

_____

_____

_____

_____

_____

_____

_____

_____

_____

_____

_____

_____

_____

-13-

BRIDGING THE GAP BETWEEN INDUSTRY, EDUCATION, AND TRAINING

When does research become relevant for application after it is completed? Does it end only after publication? Do you include stakeholders in the process?

Education is where you learn theoretical and sometimes practical aspects of what you need to do. Training, on the other hand, is where you learn the technical and very hands-on skills required for the practical aspects of your work (direct to the industry in terms of core things to be a more fruitful employer/ employee). Education teaches you why, while training teaches you how—how to do something versus the theory behind it. Combining the two will provide total human giftedness. Your resumé should read for itself, but when you have to read it to prove beyond a reasonable doubt what you can do, something isn't right.

I would like to continue to make it clear that education is good and must be pursued. As such teachings are not only for achieving status in your designated area of study, but also for broadening your mind and toughening yourself to become whom you have to be. School (and or education) is not just about learning specific skills or knowledge. School is also about teaching, pushing, and showing people how to think and analyze. It is about building mental capacity. It is also about learning to enjoy and be curious, and learning to function in society (which is social skills). Education is not just about acquiring a skill. Learning itself can be an enjoyable activity that makes people feel better and more capable.

With that said, let's also face it, what do all of Pythagoras's theorems we were forced to learn have to do with our daily life? I know NASA or Maxar technology scientists probably use these every day, but not so with some of us unfortunately. I have never seen them in any work experience directly. Well, some may argue mathematical theorems come subliminally along life's stages. Okay, what about quadratic equations that I almost nearly failed? Probably my slight hurt is that this approximately determined whether I was regarded as super-intelligent or an average student at the time. There are many more classes and programs out there that may not be relevant to what the world needs in this day and age but are still being taught. It's about time to interrogate what people study in schools and how that relates directly to industry needs, especially in these times of massive technological advancement. While most studies are relevant, a few may not be—this is the reason some institutions that understand the circumstance take advantage of the situation and carve a niche for themselves, making a name as a result.

Such institutions are able to turn education into training, where some top executives are occasionally invited into classrooms—versed in a wealth of knowledge and in touch with the current world—to transform student mindsets for progress. Such occasional visits are necessary, let's face it. Educators provide the mental capacity to adapt to a work environment, learn, and develop. Even the most successful entrepreneurs employ many graduates to run the nuts and bolts of their businesses. For example, the Walton family required an accountant, a transfer pricing economist, and engineers (all trained by universities/

colleges) for their empire business to grow and be where it is today. A combination of the theory and the practical aspects, therefore, makes education complete. Most importantly, most technological innovations have their genesis in academic research in universities/colleges rather than from the workplace. This is the reason the title of this book is *Beyond the Credentials*.

I also noted that some people get educated in traditional schools but require training on the job or in professional institutions after leaving traditional schools to help expand their mental capacity. Getting an education is not just to reflect the acquisition of skill or skills but can also reflect one's tenacity, determination, and drive to succeed.

The point is, we need to amend some of the old ways of doing things since they have long ago become obsolete. However, some schools are still living on past glories and not adding any value. As a result, students graduate and aren't able to get the right jobs. And even if they do, they aren't able to compete with others on a global basis—they tend to become liabilities, as they needed to be trained from scratch as if they have never been educated. Yes, they may have book knowledge but they have not been trained directly for the job in question. To see actual change, schools need to reduce unemployment for graduates. Increase educational quality and programs in such institutions.

Beyond the academics, beyond the credentials and book knowledge, and beyond the attainments and recognitions, people need to know the cultural dynamics of the world, and to experience the presence of executives who have come to provide practical direction on how things are done out there in addition to standard lecturing. Instead, some institutions continue to chase titles alone which is critical for validity—but not enough. I know this is not the case in some institutions, but this is an opportunity to throw light on where we need to be as a society.

I was privileged to spend time at one of the biggest supply chain facilities when I met a young woman who was working as a supervisor. We engaged in a short conversation as I was interested to know why she chose what she was doing. She was gracious enough to tell me the entire story of how she came there as a warehouse worker, packing items into boxes, and then in no time was elevated and trained to become a supervisor within the week she was hired and had been in that position for almost four months until the time of our conversation. The best part: She saw an internal opportunity for a human resource (H.R.) position, and despite holding zero degrees, she tried it anyway. She was given a chance to join the H.R. team, regardless of her zero degrees. I was super excited for her, considering her story. She was hard-working and determined not to allow anything, anyone, her condition, or her zero degrees to deter her from moving forward.

I congratulated her and wished her well. After we said our goodbyes and we both went our separate ways, one thing struck my mind—What happens to all of those who continue to write proposals upon proposals, send resumé upon resumé, and possess the right degrees and accumulated student loan debts at their back, who are trying to get the same job? What happens to all the education, credentials, and certificates others possess? While I was genuinely enthused for this passionate woman, I was a bit concerned too for others with all the degrees but with no experience. I also understand why it becomes difficult for institutions to pick someone from outside its facilities to fill open roles when they could fill them with internal people.

The reason being, the internal folks understand the processes, the rules, the dynamics, and every nuance there needs to be, as compared to a new hire with only degrees under their sleeves. I also understand that, while probably this woman cannot go and work as an AI engineer, accountant, company doctor, or company lawyer for that same institution without the relevant education and certification along with the experience, she was given a chance in H.R. No disrespect to H.R., because there are levels one needs to attain to perform at a higher level with specialized certifications that come with it, but on the other hand, while sharing my thoughts on this topic, someone said, basic H.R. is a general area where most people with common sense and a little training can function mainly at the primary level, so it wasn't surprising she got that role. Fair point?

I did engage with my nuclear family while on this project. So, when I asked my first son, SJ, what he thinks about linking credentials to success, he immediately asserted, "Daddy, what one needs is paying attention and learning"—his exact words, which connect to the story above. Imagine if the woman was not hard-working and not paying attention to details, but had all the credentials and applied for the H.R. position—she may still get the job, but it may be on a much steeper hill. May this not be misconstrued as an indication that not having credentials but working hard alone is what you need to succeed. A combination of both is essential. I want to use training so we can see the other side of life, since too much focus has been placed on academic credentials and other accolades (which are necessary) to make it to the top. It is also true that experience and mental capacity counts most. That is why many companies do aptitude and personality tests and hire people irrespective of their degrees and train them on the job depending on the role. They want to be sure the person has the mental capacity and personality to function effectively. It is ironic, however, that sometimes we strive to attain all the education, gain all the credentials and do anything we can to work for those with little or no education, or best, college dropouts. The truth is, not everyone is born to be an entrepreneur (it is a calling, and so it is with other professions). They have tenacity, coupled with opportunities to do what the average won't do—this is how, regardless of their level of educational pedigree, they succeed. We should do even better. To counter my point, it is not ironic, and there is nothing wrong or shocking about an educated person working for a college drop out. Not everyone can be and should be an entrepreneur. Many businesses founded by dropouts can't function and grow if they employ only dropouts. Do you see the reason for the balance needed in both areas?

To be globally competitive, we must be globally competent. You cannot continue doing the same old things and expect the same result, or in other words, be competitive in today's world. It is necessary, therefore, to embrace new ideas and acquire additional skills along with your core competence to make it.

Consider infusing 'Art' into Life—Science versus Art. The science part of life is where one uses everything they have been taught in the classroom and practices it on the job or life's journey. These segments of people are highly technically knowledgeable under their area of expertise—considering nobody, not even the smartest person on the planet, knows everything, not even 1% of the knowledge available. Nonetheless, they end up getting first classes in their education, and may be recognized in every subject they take, receiving several awards and credentials along the way. Who doesn't want this? We all need each other, regardless.

On the other hand, those who possess the 'Art' part of life are those who may be regarded as people who have learned to eat with queens and kings and in a village, to put it metaphorically. They know how to dress and speak, and are confident in what they do. They possess social, ethical and street wisdom beyond their credentials. They know when to speak and how to say no or yes to certain things, depending on how they are presented. They are mostly polished, sensitive, and environmentally clever. They think above their generation and are eager to learn from the street and in the boardroom. They see beauty differently from the average, and they fit into society very well. Metaphorically, they know how to dance to the tune that is being played and they do not miss any steps, to say less.

A combination of both the science and the art parts of life may position you better than just having one aspect.

For example, the days of focusing just on science, technology, engineering, and mathematics are far gone. There is the need to infuse and integrate 'Art' into it—moving from STEM to STE'A'M—Adding beauty, 'Art,' feelings, and emotions into creativity and combining the technical aspect to provide completeness. This is also mainly for engineers. As an example, I was speaking to an engineering group recently and my focus was on the above. Leaving the client with a beautiful engineering drawing without paying attention to the position of lights, dining table, colors, placement of bulbs, the arrangement of chairs, as an example, is not acceptable. In essence, it should all be factored within the building and into the designs.

In his book *The Design of Everyday Things*, Don Norman, American researcher, professor, and author, described how design serves as the communication between object and user and how to optimize that conduit of contact to make the experience of using the object pleasurable. One of the central premises of the book is that although people are often keen to blame themselves when objects appear to malfunction, it is not the fault of the user but rather the lack of intuitive guidance that should be present in the design. Norman uses case studies to describe the psychology behind what he deems good and bad design and proposes design principles.

I am also not expecting one person to know it all, and so the reason for collaboration. Moving from satisfaction to benefits and desires is the call—give the customer an unforgettable taste beyond satisfaction. Move beyond technical expertise to artistic happiness, joy, and complete human emotion when you create an experience. This is a new life.

Let's face it, jobs that are or used to be safe are now what we call 'oxymoron'—be thinking of CREATIVITY in every aspect of your passion! Where is the art in your presentation or performance? Where is it in your report, and how can it be found in your speech? Every profession has its part to play. Every country leader must adhere too. We all need it.

As a business executive, a professor, a student, or a busy person, regardless of your profession, consider making use of a calendar to manage your projects, life, and business effectively. It helps put you together and makes you look smarter than you know. It will help you organize properly and be prepared at all times for any engagement. Credentials won't write your plans for you, but they can add to your know-how in presentation.

When attending an interview for a job or meeting an investor, after organizing yourself (depends on which kind), consider the type and color of attire to wear: The type of footwear and how tight or loose the clothing on you, must all to be calculated. We have specific colors that are meant for every event and not fit for different occasions for business settings. What if you are meeting at a golf course to play golf and discuss business? You can lose business regardless of your credentials just by your appearance and presentation, including how you talk and dress. Spend time studying the type of business and people you are meeting to determine what to wear. Let your career be more significant than your dream—it takes persistence, focus, attention to detail, patience, diligence, honor, respect, and grace to follow through.

• Food for thought:

You can have perfect scores on your SATs and work hard on the job, but that alone will not fill you to the brim; it can pay your rent or pay your mortgage but not your happiness. It will not address your needs per se—add 'oomph'—so make every experience an education and every education an experience. And please, get the needed knowledge and training and add social etiquette to it.

Worksheet:

Does it matter if you have only credentials or education to climb the ladder? Or do you need both to realize the entire circumference of life's path? What is missing in your career path?

_____

_____

_____

_____

_____

_____

_____

_____

_____

_____

_____

_____

_____

_____

_____

_____

–14–

HUMAN RELATION

Building relationships and keeping them is one of the biggest assets one can have—don't burn your bridges as many people do. This is also in no way suggesting keeping people around your space who add no single value to you and deploy negative spirit around you—don't hesitate to discard such people with the speed of light.

Research reveals that the rising incidence of anxiety, depression, frustration, fear, and other mental problems are the result of a lack of close human relationships. Talking to a close friend or relative helps in releasing mental as well as physical stress.

A friend once told me he values human relations so much that, when he has the opportunity to choose between a business versus human relationship, he will choose the latter. This was echoed differently with the same meaning when one of my former bosses reiterated that, in an article he read a while ago, human relations were said to be the top-most element for success amongst others, such as laid down goals, metrics, and measurements for different projects.

Consider this: We are born into the world vulnerable, weak, and in need of physical and emotional nurturing. We also leave the world vulnerable and weak and, just as we reach out for support from those around us in infancy, so it is when we get old and frail. The level of support we get will often be based on the strength of the relationships we have created throughout our lives. The years between birth and death spent growing, learning, creating an experience, and seeing our life carried forward through our children or those we touch are characterized by the same need for interdependence. According to an article on the website socialworker.com with analysis focused on teachers, the best social worker students, practitioners, and teachers are not those who are encyclopedic in their knowledge or flawless in their technique (if there could be such a thing), but those who show that everyone they meet is the center of their universe at that moment. When we do that, we create and strengthen relationships, and our goals are met. May we always look into the eyes of our clients or students and see that beyond what they are asking at the moment, what they want more than anything else is a connection.

We were all created as social beings to connect, interact, love each other, and live a life of peace and harmony. A perfect world! We have, however, chosen to remove some elements of our relationships, leading to the problems we face today. Why don't we choose to ignore all the materialism and the stuff that makes us stressed out and unhappy, and focus instead on our relationships?

On a study from huffpost.com's website on human relationships, it was highlighted that, for a relationship to work well—in other words, to be able to synchronize trust, transparency, honesty, respect and communicate with one another—one needs a cohesive force to bring and keep these attributes together. Learn to build excellent relationships at all levels—top, bottom, lateral, and diagonal, and do not limit yourself to only those from whom you expect something. Let it be mutual, civil, and genuine.

"If civilization is to survive, we must cultivate the science of human relationships—the ability of all peoples, of all kinds, to live together, in the same world at peace."

- Franklin D. Roosevelt -

Don't burn bridges. The bridges you burn on your way out could be the very bridges that might become essential when you need to return to pick up something very crucial in life. The bolts and nuts that you unscrew and throw away might be the very bolts and nuts you might need to be able to re-screw a few things when you find yourself in another life. What binds us together is far more than what divides us. Watch out in heated moments, because the eyes you pluck out may be the very eyes you need to guide you tomorrow. The legs you break may be the legs you need to lead you tomorrow. The hands you damage may be the hands you need to help you reach something tomorrow. The mouth you slap may be the mouth and the lips you need tomorrow to speak wisdom on your behalf. Though metaphorical, let these words of wisdom guide you in everyday living.

Humans will always have their differences, but we should not allow such differences to become weapons in our hands. Don't look down on anyone by virtue of where society might have placed them today. You should also treat people with respect, as your angel might be next to you, only without wearing white robes and wings at their back. And note this— beyond talents and skills are also buried the values of honor, integrity, credibility, and how you position yourself in society to be seen positively.

Respect everyone and learn to work with everyone, if you can. We all need each other, and we don't need to physically look the same or be doing the same things to get to our desired destination. What is essential is to have a common goal. Strategies may be different, which should often be the case, but with one goal and a common purpose we can all arrive safely and on time.

I have studied a lot regarding this subject matter with the hope of presenting realistic, modern, and culturally fit and accepted norms for easy understanding. When I came across another study conducted on the reason personal relationships are essential, by contributor Mary Jo Kreitzer, R.N., Ph.D. and reviewed by Kate Hathaway, Ph.D., I noted they assessed healthy relationships as a vital component of health and wellbeing. There is compelling evidence that strong relationships contribute to a long, healthy, and happy life. Conversely, the health risks from being alone or isolated in one's life are comparable to the risks associated with cigarette smoking, blood pressure, and obesity.

Research also shows that healthy relationships can help you in the following areas:

Dealing with stress:

The support offered by a caring friend can provide a buffer against the effects of stress. In a study of over 100 people, researchers found that people who completed a stressful task experienced a faster recovery when they were reminded of people with whom they had strong relationships with. Those who were reminded of stressful relationships, on the other hand, experienced even more stress and higher blood pressure.

Being healthier:

Strong relationships contribute to health at any age. According to psychologist Sheldon Cohen, college students who reported having strong relationships were half as likely to catch a common cold when exposed to the virus. At the same time, an AARP study with older adults found that loneliness is a significant predictor of poor health. More generally, a 2012 international Gallup poll in the United States found that people who feel they have friends and family to count on are usually more satisfied with their health than people who feel isolated.

Moreover, hanging out with healthy people increases your likelihood of health. In their book *Connected*, Christakis and Fowler show that non-obese people are more likely to have non-obese friends because healthy habits spread through our social networks—this too is the power of commonality.

Living longer:

It is believed that people with strong social relationships are 50% less likely to die prematurely. Similarly, Dan Buettner's Blue Zones research calculates that committing to a life partner can add three years to life expectancy. According to Nicholas Christakis and James Fowler, men's life expectancies benefits from marriage more than women's do. Whatever the case is, it is because of human relationships.

Feeling richer:

A survey by the National Bureau of Economic Research of 5,000 people found that doubling your group of friends has the same effect on your wellbeing as a 50% increase in income! Regardless of what technology has done to us by replacing personal interaction with people with FaceTime and the use of other gadgets to connect, physical meeting and interaction remain more powerful—except for rare occasions like the COVID-19 pandemic, during which it became necessary to be physically distant from one another. Let's also face the fact that technology has tremendously increased relationships across the globe. Consider Twitter, LinkedIn, Zoom, Skype, Google Hangouts, and many more tools that have come to improve and transform the way we communicate and relate to one another across borders with ease. Nevertheless, in person interaction cannot be replaced with gadgets and technology. Let's encourage it when it becomes necessary.

Do not relent in doing good. Continuously sow into people. Though the benefits may not come to you directly, continue to do your part because, in so doing, someone is also being prepared for you through another means. We don't need credentials to relate to one another in peace. We need common sense, mutual respect, acceptance, and belief that all men are created equal, and it's about time we treat each other with the dignity each person deserves.

A woman who worked as a temporary worker hoping to transition to full-time at a big company with locations all over the globe was stunned about an incident. She worked smart and hard, solving problems that were difficult to crack. Problems that existed for over three years until she arrived. This woman was able to resolve those issues within two months of being hired. She was able to create efficient pathways to deal with customers and a sound system for monitoring. When it was time for her to leave (because she wasn't offered the permanent position), she was treated like a rug. The H.R. came into the office late on a Friday while she was getting ready to be picked up by her spouse, only to be informed that it was her last day in the office. No human empathy and respect were exhibited at all. The H.R. stood in front of this woman and kept demanding the company's computer, as though she was a criminal, until she packed everything and left. This poor woman with a frustrated look and shock in her face asked why she was treated that way. "I thought I had created a healthy relationship with you guys to demand at least a day's notice," she alleged. The only answer the H.R. gave was, "It is company policy." Company policy?

What type of company policy is so cruel and disrespectful to human beings when nothing criminal has occurred? Was it her personal policy that was enacted into the company policy? People are weird. This is an absolute disregard for human dignity and could discourage hard, smart and sincere work when another opportunity is presented to this woman again, who now has the notion that no one cares. This should be a wakeup call to companies and leaders that treat people like rugs.

• Food for thought:

Most organizations employ a total—person approach. This approach recognizes that an organization does not just hire someone with skills, but rather the whole person. This person not only comes with biases, personal challenges, and soft and technical skills, but also comes with experiences and assumes a sense of authority and respect. By looking at a person from this perspective, an organization can begin to understand that what happens to an employee outside of work can affect their job performance, a reality observed in a study by the website saylordot.org on human relations.

Just as the climbing lianas and the redwood trees rely on one another's support systems to succeed, one cannot do without others.

Worksheet:

The phrase human relationship is even more important than knowledge—to what extent do you see it so?

_____

_____

_____

_____

Do you agree or disagree that human relations are crucial in anything you do? Explain your answer.

_____

_____

_____

_____

Even though I understand that people can be weird, we still have to live alongside with them with tact! Share what ticks you off and prevents you from having a good relationship with someone.

_____

_____

_____

_____

-15-

COMMUNICATION – NOT WHAT BUT HOW

Communication, in general, is key to successful living. Oh no, let me correct myself! Effective communication is what I mean. Communication, in other words, is the lifeblood to a prosperous relationship—be it an institutional, group, or personal development. Imagine having zero or less communication in an intimate setting, or between business partners, friends, or acquaintances. How will that work? Consider also no adequate communication direction established in an institution for guidance on what to do and how to do jobs properly—what will be the result of that institution? Mere speeches or just chatting or talking without absolute direction to specific tasks are exempted. We are, here, referring to real statements. Someone can be with you for a long time and constantly chatting, but not having real communication or conversation with you. Nothing new revealed. Communication must be efficient, effective, direct, and something that produces expected results. Your part might be to listen while others respond, or to engage in a dialogue when necessary. Whether for social, business, or relationship-building reasons, engage in real conversation with a purpose in mind, being aware that communication serves a greater proportion to their sustenance. Bear in mind that people could be heard but not listened to, people are reading but may not be reasoning, therefore making no impact—which part are you?

"The most important thing in communication is listening to what isn't said"

- Peter Drucker -

Communication, be it business or personal, mostly, is to make an impact and create an action point. Also, it is to move someone to action. See communication as unique to every family, culture, country, and, of course, institution. It is like a musical instrument that is being conducted to get the desired result and sound. The conductor leads while every other person orchestrates their part for a harmonious melody—a perfect result.

According to an article on Michael Page's executive search website regarding the importance of excellent communication, they observed three critical areas summarized below:

- *Choose the appropriate medium* - While face-to-face communication is the most straightforward way of discussing topics with your team, it isn't always an option. It is vital to figure out what you are going to say, and why, and that you choose the right medium. Take time to decide if an email, telephone call, or memo is the best way to get your message across.

- *Keep everyone involved* - If you want effective communication to run throughout the entire office and your environment, you need to be accessible. Make sure that the lines of communication are kept open at all times. It will encourage people to open dialogue with you regularly. This is particularly important when dealing with remote staff.

- *Listen to your team members* - The ability to listen to your colleagues and take any suggestions or feedback that they give seriously is crucial. Real listening shows respect and allows you to learn about any outstanding issues you may need to address as an employer.

Active listening is also part of communication. Talking, directing, instructing, and always being at the center of decision making isn't the only way of communicating. It has to be a two or more way process. The most effective is the power of listening, empathizing, and paying close attention to what you are being told—and what is not being said, because that might even be louder.

Communicating can also be seen as a form of science and or art—Science in the sense that what you know and learn is that which you're ready to defend. This is factual and verifiable. For example, as a gatekeeper, the protocol directs you to ask everyone entering the building if they are twenty-one years of age before giving them access. Even if they have grey hairs, you still insist on asking them about their age and want to see their ID card—what sense does that make? Avoid being a robot. Yes, we need the science part of communication to prepare for the rule of law and laid down principles to be enforced, but without the 'art' form, it is fruitless. By applying common sense and the use of art in thinking and reasoning, you can jump over obvious questions.

On the other hand, the art part comes to add wisdom to the science form of communication. On the same hypothetical example stated earlier, though the protocol insists on asking everyone their age to make sure minors aren't admitted into the building, by using common sense you will be able to ignore certain aspects. Ignoring that aspect of questioning an older person about their age to determine if they are minor when it is obvious the person coming is frail and holding a walking stick is the use of the art form of communication. The list of questions is just a guide for you.

There are different styles of communication. People get surprised after presenting an excellent proposal to groups of expected investors or potential employer with high hopes and receiving negative results. It sends disappointed waves down their spines. Of course, maybe someone else did better than you, or it may be because your presentation was not well received—be it written or verbal. In my McKinsey & Company Fellowship training, it is believed that when communicating with different people, study their credentials, titles, and backgrounds to tailor your communication to make the desired impact. For example, when interacting with the following experts, adopt the indicated strategies:

- *Marketers* - use more charts. They are more attuned to charts than anything else, so use these to explain your viewpoint.
- *Finance gurus* - use more financial figures. They love numbers and using them will portray you as smart and make you be seen as someone who knows what you are talking about.
- *Operational folks* - use more process content. For people in my type of caliber who are deep thinkers and process-oriented, gravitate towards showing how you arrived at a solution rather than just stating the solution. They would have questions in their minds like, which path did you take, and what were the lessons learned?
- *The Millennial and younger generation* - adapt more to social media and text messaging regardless of the message unless in a work environment or situations

where there is no choice but physical gathering becomes necessary. Using standard TV screens are not effective tools to reach these groups; phones, YouTube, and anything they can assess quickly on their handsets are more effective reaching tools. I was not the right social media user until I wrote my first book—and even now, I am still comparatively behind.

The above is not a suggestion that marketers do not want to hear about figures. Yes, they do. Neither am I saying that finance folks aren't interested in charts. They sure are. Operational guys are also not only interested in process conversation. The point here is to help you know where to focus your energy, especially in the short amount of time presented to you to make the desired impact mostly in business context. The reason is simple: Finance gurus are biased towards numbers, and so are the rest towards their area of interest. Imagine telling a finance guru about the stock market and how market share is expected to rise in a particular segment by 5% in the coming year. How smart will that person see you?

You will then be given a platform (not necessarily a physical stage but an attention stage) to expand on your hypothesis and theory. You can now (depending on the time allotted, within which you must stick to) showcase your knowledge. At that point, you can add charts and processes but pay heavy attention to numbers to catch that finance guru's attention. That's how it is done. The trick works. It's not a trick in that sense; it is common sense applied through wisdom—the same way with a marketer or an operational expert. Flip the strategy based on what interests them first. Then attention will naturally be created, which allows you to loop in other information. This is about choosing the right tool for the right person. You can connect the right person to the wrong tool, thereby making the person look like a 'jerk' on their job. The person is not a jerk. It is because there is no alignment, and so it is with communication. If you want to get the right impact, find the right medium. Others who may not be privileged to this type of unique information may be burning the candles overnight, hoping upon hope for a miracle. Yes, miracles can always occur, but while on earth there is also wisdom available to apply—spare that miracle for another day, or something more precious. Apply knowledge and wisdom to your communication, instead of just rattling.

Millennials, Gen Y's, X's, or Z's as indicated, love social media and text messaging. If you want to reach the mass in this group, don't spend too much time sending emails. Simple use of targeted social media will do the magic. It is not to say they don't read or use emails, but it is the level of impact that you want to make that matters. No wonder some marketing institutions (be it internal or outsource ones) may be struggling due to their wrong choice of offerings in the marketplace. Times have changed, and so must communication. For our children who are regarded in the Linksters generation, I can't imagine what to use to communicate with them in the future. But guess what, the head is on the neck for a reason—when it gets there, we will cross that 'river' too.

• Food for thought:

Stories sell, facts tell. Repetitiveness in key lines is remembered more than facts. Consider the famous *I have a dream* line from Martin Luther King Jr's great speech. This has become a viral and well-known line over five decades, and still resonates. This became possible due to the nature of the platform given to sell an idea, product, service, or yourself. MLK took advantage of this and did just that. Most people may not recall the other actual lines that preceded before and after, but everyone remembers the tag line— "I have a dream." This doesn't work when you need to capture someone's attention for a quick second, especially when you're not a known figure.

Final tip—in business communication, when you're copied (cc) or blind copied (bcc), for example, in an email trail, you're technically not supposed to be responding to that email. Allow the one to which it is being sent to, to respond first. The reasoning is that you're only being notified of the message. These little tips help one surge ahead of the curve in society, as far as communication on a high level is concerned.

Worksheet:

Share your communication style with people at the workplace, social places, and with colleagues and family. What do you consider necessary in communication, considering the ideas shared in the chapter?

_____

_____

_____

_____

_____

_____

_____

_____

_____

_____

_____

_____

_____

_____

_____

–16–

INTEGRITY

The word integrity and its expected action are priceless. It is about reliability and making sure you do what you say you'll do even if it is hard to do. In other words, when you say you'll do something, do it—that's it. We shouldn't over-embellish the meaning of integrity. As simple as it is, it takes guts, credibility, focus, respect of yourself and others, honoring the time and consistency to make it a reality.

> *"Real integrity is doing the right thing, knowing that nobody's going to know whether you did it or not."*
>
> *- Oprah Winfrey -*

Integrity is about doing the right thing because it's the right thing to do regardless of the outcome. It is not an easy path or road to take if you truly want to stay loyal to what is right—however, it is worth it if you do. You may not be a popular figure among your peers for taking this course, but staying true to your instincts for the long haul is worth more than money can buy. Leaders who practice the course of integrity may not be the most famous or flashy among leaders, but at the end of the road, their labor will not go without notice.

Whenever the opportunity presents itself for me to hire someone to perform a specific duty, one of the critical things I look out for beyond their credentials is someone who is loyal, trustable and reliable, someone who can indeed stay the course of what they are saying beyond what they have written in their resumé. I look for someone who is ready to learn and be honest, but most importantly someone who has passion and integrity.

Aside from watching out for their actions, when speaking with the potential candidate, I also watch out for the eyes, as they reveal if someone is telling the truth. I watch out for the blinks, facial expressions, and many other subtle acts to make my decision. Some people are good at hiding their feelings, but they are only an exceptional minority. In front of me are their credentials, resumé claiming their capabilities, and certificates. Knowing vividly that asking them questions directly to the resumé will produce what they might have rehearsed to tell me, I usually swing off the script and ask basic and straightforward questions that are practical to determine the pin I am looking for in the haystack. Let me not be mistaken, I do ask questions about their resumé, but I do not dwell on it too much.

I also love the situation where I will ask the potential employee to work with the institution for a day or two to assess other ways of how they perform—observing their leadership style, temperament, and how they work under pressure with less supervision. That strategy is more powerful than what is written on the resumé or bio. I understand you cannot get information from the person within a day or two, not even within the standard three months probationary period. Still, it gives you some sense of their work ethic, how they relate to others, and their general way of seeing things. Imagine someone telling you on their resumé they can type five hundred words in two minutes, only to test the person and it is taking more than ten minutes to get the same number of words and with lots of mistakes—that reveals true character, integrity and performance. Please understand we are not looking for angels, but at least someone with clear conscience and honor, someone who is quick to think on their feet but slow to speak—considering we also have different types of people and no one person is the same. The work type must also be considered.

"Perhaps the surest test of an individual's integrity is his refusal to do or say anything that would damage his self-respect."

- Thomas S. Monson -

You cannot betray someone's invested trust in you. Being someone with high credibility and integrity can take you far as you may be regarded as trustworthy.

With thanks to the website yourdictionary.com for some of the excerpts, let's consider a few of the expected integrity points summarized for *everyday living*:

- Return money that you noticed someone dropped without expecting a reward
- When in a serious relationship, don't keep secrets from each other
- If someone gives you confidential information, never tell anyone
- Go back to the store and pay for something you forgot to pay for
- Do not let someone else take the blame for something you did
- Inform the cashier he gave you too much change back
- Never betray a friend's trust even if you get in trouble
- Keep your promises even if it takes extra effort
- Do not gossip or talk badly about someone

Let's consider a few expected integrities in the Workplace:

- If you are in management, keep your employees informed, so they will know what is coming and what needs to be done

- If your company asks you to do something against your code of conduct, refuse it. If it means losing a good-paying job, so be it. Find a more ethical company to work for

- Work when you are supposed to and save socializing, snacking, searching on the internet and receiving and making personal phone calls unless under critical situations

- When making a business deal, make sure everything is on the table, and nothing is left out

- Adhere to company policies and procedures and be responsible. Do what you say you'll do

- Show respect and empathy to coworkers with appropriate conversations

- If you make a mistake and a team's project gets messed up, or you miss a deadline, own up to your mistake. Don't let teammates take the fall

- Work together as a team. This builds trust and shows integrity

- If you find yourself in a conflict-of-interest situation, get out of it as soon as possible

- Don't accept the praise for someone else's work. That includes stealing someone's idea or pretending to have worked on a successful project

Consider also the following general ones:

- As parents or if you are responsible for someone, when you go too far, learn to apologize to your kids, nieces, nephews, or dependents for over-punishing or yelling at them—they will listen and respect you back
- People in positions of power apologizing for keeping their audience waiting would show respect to them
- Anyone giving another person the benefit of the doubt when the circumstances are unclear—gives them second chances
- Showing respect to everyone regardless of the person's origin, the tone of their skin, religious belief or social orientation
- Offering to help others in need, especially in difficult times
- Putting others' needs above your own
- Taking responsibility for your actions
- Being trustworthy and accountable
- Being authentic and responsible
- Valuing another person's time

"You are in integrity when the life you are living on the outside matches who you are on the inside."

- Alan Cohen -

When you notice that someone is experiencing something troubling beyond their capability, do your best to assist them with their situation as best as you can—this is true integrity. This is correlated to trust and loyalty as well. Loyalty requires a person to put their personal needs or goals on the side, so they can do what is required of them. Loyalty is manifested internally first—being loyal to 'you' first is more powerful because it helps you be loyal to others. Trust comes in handy when you're needed most. If someone tells you 'I trust you,' it's a good burden to carry—hold it tight and cherish it like an award from the Emmys.

||||||||||||||||||||||||||||||||||||||||||||||||||||||||||||||||||||||||||||||||||||||||||||||||||||||||||||||||||||||||||||||||||||||||||

• Food for thought:

Great leaders never compromise their honesty and integrity by cheating. They are attuned to the core values that guide them. Are you one?

"One of the truest tests of integrity is its blunt refusal to be compromised."

- Chinua Achebe -

You need to be emotionally intuitive by not living as if you are the only important person in the world, not caring for the well-being of others, be it physical or emotional. When you have true integrity, you are more attuned to the world and those around you. You do not live in your little bubble but allow yourself to be part of everyone else's. It's one of the best investments one can make in life. Its fruits transcend generations and do not fall under the standard stock exchange inflationary servitude.

Worksheet:

Integrity may be a fancy word but it is not easily practiced.
In what ways can you improve your integrity?

_____

_____

_____

_____

_____

_____

_____

_____

_____

_____

_____

_____

_____

_____

_____

_____

What practical ways can you infuse integrity as a way of life rather than seeing it as a chore?

_____

_____

_____

_____

_____

_____

_____

_____

_____

_____

_____

_____

_____

_____

_____

_____

_____

–17–

REPUTATIONAL CAPITAL

"It takes many good deeds to build a good reputation, and only one bad one to lose it."

- Benjamin Franklin -

While some people seek financial capital, others seek reputational capital to surge. Money is not everything. What do you profit if you have all the wealth—the houses, ranches, horses, private jets, the most luxurious cars, and everything that comes with it—and have no reputation or respect to connect the final dots? By the way, the things I mentioned are the very things I am gearing towards, so don't be deceived; those things (once you can afford them) are great to have—however, add reputation, which then becomes a massive capital for you.

Integrity, reputation, and respect are essential tools to have, so it is an expectation from the one who owns them to give them to others as well. Both parties must keep their subliminal promises and deliver them as expected.

According to an article featured on the website selfgrowth. com, your reputation capital is the brand your name carries— the sum of your good name, good works, and your history. As an individual, your reputation and the image it carries are essential. With every move you make, you are validating in the eyes of your family, friends, neighbors, and business colleagues the image consistency of your reputation. Understanding that your actions and behavior translate into your reputation is important!

This article went on to state that skills, credentials, experience all together contribute to one's professional reputation; however, these categories alone do not determine one's reputation. The intangibles of what you bring to a job—your reputation—matter as well. As a consultant or a person, your name is your brand.

They continued to say that reputation is not an intangible asset but rather a bankable asset. An excellent reputation creates demand, and demand can command premium pricing. A good reputation will also define the expectation of everything you offer, whether you are a one-person consulting firm or a large organization—I agree. An individual or organization's reputation is a fragile quality that is challenging to earn but easy to lose.

The most effective form of marketing is still word-of-mouth referrals, and that relies entirely on reputation—be it real or perceived—from what I know. Some would argue that knowledge is your most valuable asset, but in reality, reputation is. Knowledge can be bought, or even sub-contracted, while reputation can't. You could know everything in the world, but if no one trusts you, you're not going to make a living with just your knowledge. Reputation is about trust, and to gain trust, you must deliver on what you promise. This is true for the individual or the organization.

Developing your reputation requires effort, and the heart and passion for making a difference, especially in the lives of others. If you are to become a person who can impact the lives of others, you must first believe in your ability to influence others, and that you can be a positive and committed force in your approach to effecting personal and organizational change. The very concept of "having a good reputation" implies that you possess a high degree of personal insight and a high degree of credibility in being able to take others to a place they have not been.

The phrase "image is everything" probably sounds familiar. But concerning reputation, it refers to more than you might expect. Each of your interactions and communications is noted by your business colleagues, friends, and family and helps shape your reputation.

To help you achieve a polished, professional reputation and image; here are some suggestions to consider:

Courtesy - Be polite and respectful because it does not only boost your image but builds consensus and helps people and projects move forward in a friendly environment. Being courteous includes listening, making realistic requests, providing constructive input, being on time, and not expecting others to solve your problems.

Seek feedback - If you're not sure what image you're projecting both on and off the job, ask a few people. Make sure you ask people who will be honest in their assessment. You may want to ask beyond family and friends. I have considered feedback from my peers and mentors to often be the most honest. You should seek information that will provide you the best direction and guidance for your image-building efforts. Feedback is a gift, one of my former bosses used to say, with a cautionary look as she said it. How can't you get it?

Be constructive - Don't gossip or spread rumors or even listen to them. If conversations are not factual or constructive, they are not good for building your reputation and professional image. Stay away from toxic people.

Work like you own it - Do not approach your job like an employee. Work like you own the company and have a personal stake in the results of your projects.

Among the research I have conducted, the above assertions were a perfect fit into what I believe to be true for mental consumption and deliberation. This is so mainly because I believe in them and they fit the exact purpose of this topic. The only trouble is, writing about this is more comfortable than applying it in real life—however, constant practice will keep you on the right path. Think it through, instead of telling yourself, "Oh, I already do this and that," instead, ask this: What can I do to be a better version of myself?

It's also critical to think of everyone as a customer, whether the person is a coworker or client. Are you easy to do business with? Some are bad customers or bad nuts to be taken out of the lot.

Make sure you identify the difference, so you don't cut off the wrong ones. It is like the wheat and the chaff. When they are in their early stages, they look almost the same, only until time passes, when they start to bear fruit. It is then that you will now clearly separate them - because only the wheat will bear fruit and not the chaff. So it is with people and their reputations.

Your greatest gifts can also become your greatest weakness. The greatest inspirer can be the worse 'cursor' in private. Be a fruit inspector. The very job you prayed to have and interviewed for with humility, after a few months on the post can also become your downfall, in that you can easily forget how you got in and begin to lure yourself over a span of control and start misbehaving. Some people build their reputation through humility, but in fact, some are built based on the upside-down of humility theory—this needs to be tested over time to draw the right conclusion. Some people are blindfolded so much that, when someone who used to provide the inspired direction over decades begins to use their selfish ambitions to craft new commands that favor them, this behavior is not quickly identified, because how can the person who inspired them be wrong all of a sudden? Open your eyes. They are also human first.

"Your gift is the number of things you do with your absolute best with the least amount of effort—identify your gift."

- Steve Harvey -

If you keep struggling over something you've been doing for some time without success, either it isn't your calling, or you need to pay extra attention to details to triumph. This is in the absence of persistence to a goal you want to achieve. Usually, when you find passion and joy in what you do, it brings you fulfillment and mostly leads to creating a lasting reputation—it comes naturally.

Building trust and reputation as capital is arguably more significant than someone liking you or anything you can think of. Someone can like you but not trust you. Someone can know you, but neither like nor trust you. You can trust someone you don't like. But above all, to be liked, known, and trusted is best—trust plays a huge role; one can work with a trusted person but not necessarily like them, but it is challenging to work with someone you like but do not trust, or someone you know but do not like. Trust is key. Trust is a reputation. Trust binds knowledge, wisdom, integrity, credibility and more together to create reputational capital.

"Who steals my purse steals trash; 'tis something, nothing; 'Twas mine, 'tis his, and has been slave to thousands; But he that filches from me my good name Robs me of that which not enriches him, and makes me poor indeed."

- William Shakespeare -

• **Food for thought:**

In all you do and in all that you invest in, also invest in reputational capital. It is sustainable, lasts, and is infectious from generation to generation. If appropriately maintained, it will sustain you. It is worth more than gold.

Worksheet:

With the knowledge of reputation as capital, share where you have lots of 'investments' (reputational capital) or where you will increase investment as far as reputation is concerned?

_____

_____

_____

_____

_____

_____

_____

_____

_____

_____

_____

_____

_____

_____

–18–

TIME MANAGEMENT, GOAL SETTING AND PLANNING (PART 1)

Time is a scarce resource, and one of the few things one cannot make but can spend. Using it wisely, therefore, will benefit you. Punctuality even in simple things like making it on time to a meeting, be it social or official, is essential.

Time management is one key aspect where you respect what it brings. What most people don't appreciate is how a delay in one element of a project could lead to delay in another, causing a negative multiplier effect. When things are done on time, systems communicate and work moves effectively and efficiently. Time is one of the scarcest resources, and needs careful management and monitoring. Someone can be on time at work but could be lazy on the job and could cause productivity loss—so managing time doesn't only mean being on time but also working with diligence, precision, and accuracy to avoid rework.

I was in the process of writing this book when I had to help guide my younger son get dressed for something I can't recall. In the process, he wasn't dressing correctly, so I was trying to correct the process he was using for efficiency and effectiveness. I actually mentioned to him that I wanted to help him be effective. Guess what he said to me? "Daddy-daddy-daddy" (his usual three times calling) "I know what effectiveness means—

being effective is about using your time wisely." I went 'woo'—because he was only six years old and was educating me so nicely. I said to my wife, I have never seen anyone give a more concise version of effectiveness than he did. It's true.

How you manage your time and how you use it reflects who you are. Respect for time can be a deal-breaker or loss of opportunities. You can do the right thing at the wrong time, and the reverse is true. In supply chain management, we call this just in time (J.I.T.)—delivering projects at the right time, not earlier or later, but at the very time it is needed. This saves institutions lots of resources. This way inventory and warehousing cost, for example, are minimized, items are received when other systems that are meant to add value are ready, and items are processed and delivered to the end customer on the day and time it is expected to—not earlier, not later. This is time management, in essence.

Setting a goal and planning is essential to one's life management. Sometimes when such words are pronounced, we think of it as meaning doing big things, but no, it is the small things you plan for, that matters. Setting a goal can be for both small and big milestones where you can measure them over a disciplined period to see if you're on track or not. Your goals should be S.M.A.R.T. (specific, measurable, achievable, realistic and timebound): I have studied several different S.M.A.R.T. goals and taught this strategy to many groups, but a summary version from the website *top achievement.com* caught my attention:

Specific:
A specific goal has a much higher chance of being accomplished than a general goal. To set a particular goal, you must answer the six "W" questions: *Who is involved? *What do I want to accomplish? *Where, to identify a location. *When,

to establish a time frame. *Which areas identify requirements and constraints? *Why—specific reasons, purpose or benefits of accomplishing the goal.

Example: A general goal would be, "Get in shape." But a specific goal would say, "Join a health club and workout three days a week."

Measurable:

Establish concrete criteria for measuring progress toward the attainment of each goal you set. When you measure your progress, you stay on track, reach your target dates, and experience the exhilaration of achievement that spurs you on to the continued effort required to reach your goal.

To determine if your goal is measurable, ask questions such as "How much? How many? How will I know when it is accomplished?"

Attainable or Achievable goals:

When you identify goals that are most important to you, you begin to figure out ways you can make them come true. You develop the attitudes, abilities, skills, and financial capacity to reach them. You start seeing previously overlooked opportunities to bring yourself closer to the achievement of your goals.

You can attain almost any goal you set when you plan your steps wisely and establish a time frame that allows you to carry out those steps. Goals that may have seemed far away and out of reach eventually move closer and become attainable, not because your goals shrink, but because you grow and expand to match them. When you list your goals, you build your self-image. You see yourself as worthy of these goals and develop the traits and personality that allow you to possess them.

Realistic:

To be realistic, a goal must represent an objective toward which you are both willing and able to work with. A goal can be both high and realistic; you are the only one who can decide just how high your goal should be. But be sure that every goal represents substantial progress.

A high goal is frequently easier to reach than a low one because a low goal exerts a low motivational force. Some of the hardest jobs you ever accomplish seem easy only because they were a labor of love.

Timely or Time-bound:

A goal should be grounded within a time frame. With no time frame tied to it, there's no sense of urgency. If you want to lose ten pounds, when do you want to lose it by? "Someday" won't work. But if you anchor it within a timeframe, "by March 17th," for example, then you've set your unconscious mind into motion to begin working on the goal. Your goal is probably realistic if you truly believe that it can be accomplished. Additional ways to know if your goal is realistic is to determine if you have accomplished anything similar in the past or ask yourself what conditions would have to exist to achieve this goal.

The 'T' can also stand for Tangible—A goal is tangible when you can experience it with one of the senses: taste, touch, smell, sight or hearing.

When your goal is tangible, you have a better chance of making it specific and measurable and thus attainable.

The above has become standard tools used by most people, but what is missing is true enforcement. Knowing something and doing it are two different things. I have met people who are knowledgeable and well-read, but they prove to have difficulty when explaining simple things. What they haven't done is to implement what they claim they know.

Planning for everything you do:

I am a heavy calendar user. Considering the amount of money that I spend on my cell phones, I make sure they better serve as executive secretaries to me. I write my plans, ideas, dreams, and visions down, and I will always make sure I discuss it with my wife as a way of being accountable. Telling someone about your plans pushes you to achieve them if you're a person of veracity.

Goal setting draws you to your vision. A vision is the ability to see things others can't see in the short-term. Usually, such a vision or goal is only for you, and only you can see it. This is the reason why you don't judge someone's behavior too quickly—you may be judging a book by the cover before you read to the end. Setting a goal and having a clear vision is a journey, and it is the work of an artist. Until they are done with their final work, you will not understand what they are doing. At the initial point, it is madness to the observer, somewhere in the middle it may start to make sense a bit, but when the final piece of art is complete, there you will see jaws dropping with admiration, clapping, and the words "Oh, I see" will start to emerge. Do not let anyone steal your vision or goal. Do not let anyone sit on it or toy with it.

–19–

TIME MANAGEMENT, GOAL SETTING AND PLANNING (PART 2)

This section of the chapter deals mainly with how precision and accuracy are understood and how to connect each or both to a goal to attain a desired result.

Precision versus accuracy dilemma:

These words are interchangeably used and misunderstood sometimes. Even some of the well-educated miss the mark on what these truly stand for. I know people are seeking the help of search engines right now while they continue to read to prove me wrong. Please bear with me to digest this. This is an area I spend more time on whenever I am wearing my consulting hat while in the field by linking it directly to a specific business development for profitability.

Let's consider three scenarios and analyze them below. We will use the meeting of a bullseye point as the target and as a success for the sake of this study. It doesn't matter if it emanates from a corporate or personal perspective—meeting your set goal is what is important.

Not precise nor accurate (see pictorial representation below):

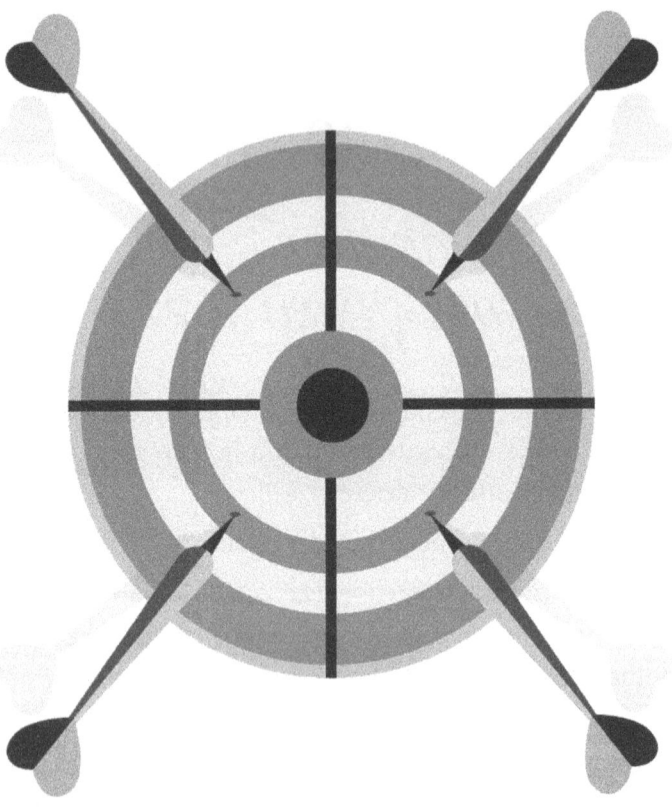

Imagine a target with a dot in the middle, the goal is to hit the bullseye in the middle but was missed on four attempts—This is an obvious miss of a goal. No one debates about the fact that you have missed the bullseye here. It is obvious here that you did not meet your goal, not even close. So, what you must do is to reassess what went wrong and do it again. One thing you should never do is never give up on your dreams if they are your calling.

Precise but not accurate (see pictorial representation below):

You have a second chance to hit the target again but this time, all of the four arrows hit a particular point but not the desired location. This is a critical area where most people fall short. The fact that you continuously arrive at a point of decision doesn't constitute its rightness. The fact that the decision is easy doesn't mean it is the right decision. We sometimes feel so comfortable in this space and almost forget where we intended to be initially. I am always concerned about this stage in life where a lot of people (or institutions) end up thinking they have arrived. After all, they are consistent and good at what they do. Yes, you may be, but being consistent or precise may not mean accuracy or your desired goal. Reassess your original goal(s)—the medical doctor you wanted to be that ended at a nurse level. The attorney you wanted to be that ended at legal clerk stage. The athlete you wanted to be that is going nowhere because you cannot wake up to exercise to be fit for it. The entrepreneur you desired to be for which you expect to learn from the best in the industry, but instead you are building someone's else's dream forever—what is yours? Consider these points carefully, take a moment to think through them, and reflect on what your next steps may be. It's not about winning an argument, or feeling better—because you can win a battle but lose a war. The fact that you win an argument doesn't mean your goals are achieved—the truth remains.

Precise and accurate (see pictorial representation below):

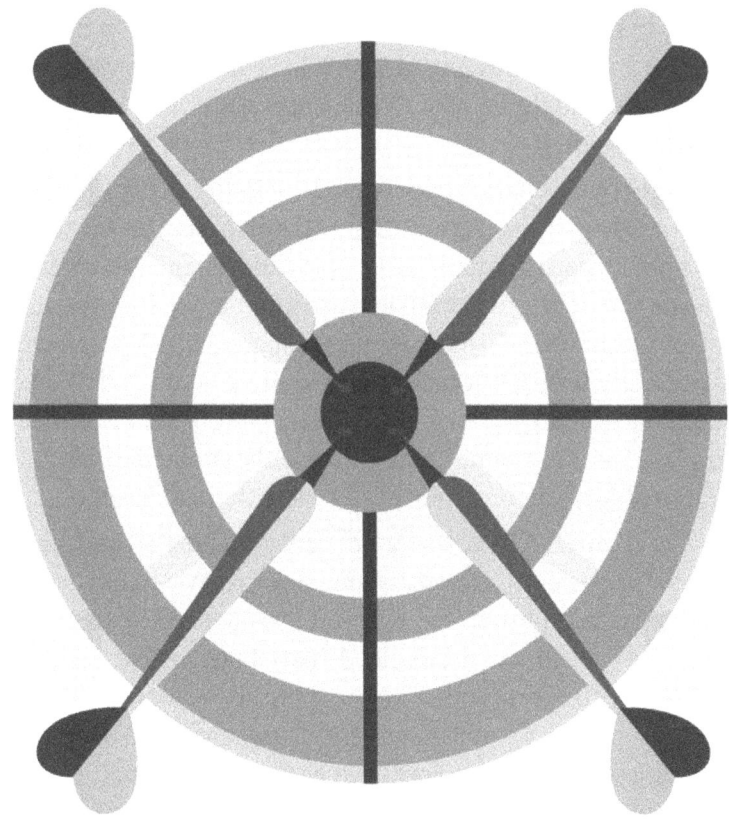

On the third attempt to hit the target, successfully, all four arrows hit the desired location. This is the perfect goal that you initially set to attain—where precision and accuracy meet. Once you hit that bullseye, you are set to go. The bullseyes, in this case, represent your KPIs in a company. It could be the exact weight loss number you set to achieve at the beginning of the year. It could be the credentials (yes, credentials) you set yourself to attain when you were young. It could be a financial breakthrough you have always desired to attain. It could be your goal to pay off that student loan. It could also represent the opportunity to start an investment pool to plan for your retirement to secure the kind of freedom you desire for yourself. Whatever it is that you plan to achieve, minus any force majeure that are beyond your control, you should be able to make it a slam dunk even if the roads are rough.

The above scenarios have helped me in some of my projects. I use them to assess accuracy on project planning, its executing, successes, progress monitoring and control measurement. I translate theories into actual deliveries and make sure there are control mechanisms laid down for sustainability. These words are not mere terms, but technical and must be treated as such. Pause and remind yourself about those pictures of Ferrari cars you placed in the room, hoping to ride them one day. Nothing is impossible if you put your head to it with no distractions.

The alignment of goals for efficiency is essential and serves as a tool for positive progress. If someone asks you to buy orange juice for them on the street, will you use an airplane to go and buy it or you will use a bicycle? What about just walking the block to buy the orange juice? Now, there are factors to consider before jumping to a conclusion—the distance and the timing are significant. The fact that you have access to an airplane, boat, bicycle, or car, should not be the reason to use any of these without analyzing the facts behind the request. This is how many people manage goals in metaphorical terms. In that sense, some people are riding a bicycle to their desired goals when they should be driving a car, while others are walking when they should be using airplanes due to the speed needed and the short time available. This is where the application of wisdom comes in. Until one adjusts the vision or tweaks the goal, how will they succeed? One needs to check back in with how S.M.A.R.T. their goals are and plan accordingly. Learn to celebrate the little deliverables that lead to significant milestones.

||||||||||||||||||||||||||||||||||||||||||||||||||||||||||||||||||||||||||||||||||||||||||||||||||||||||||||||||||||||||||||||||||||||||||||||||||||||||||||||||||||||||||||||||||||||||

• Food for thought:

While credentials are vital, critical attention to the original goal is what will take you to the top. Imagine professionals like pilots or surgeons who cannot make one single mistake for any excuse— imagine they give the excuse of only being precise but not combining precision with accuracy—the result will land people to an early death. This applies to businesses, be it personal, multinational, or working with a small institution in a community, such as a school. Genuine mistakes are necessary tools for perfection, but unacceptable in certain professions.

Worksheet:

Share your goals using the S.M.A.R.T module as a practice.

_____

_____

_____

_____

_____

_____

_____

When we say, 'time management,' what does it mean to you?

_____

_____

_____

_____

_____

_____

_____

_____

_____

-20-

CONTROL OVER TIME AND MONEY

The reason I work hard and smart is to have six Saturdays in the week and only one Sunday in the near future—this is called freedom! This is how I want to live my life in a few years to come. This metaphor and reality is only possible when you have control over time and money. Every day becomes a weekend for you because you don't see the difference. A respectable man I know usually says, whenever he wakes up, he often doesn't know which day of the week it is until he goes to the shopping mall—the number of people in the shop will determine which day of the week it is. Those who are in a 9-5 job are mostly in long lines after work or weekends shopping. In reverse, the rich and those who have the freedom I am describing shop during the week when no one is around.

When someone tells you they don't have any help or money for you when you need it most, three things could be happening;

1. Some of them may be telling the truth to the very core.
2. Others may also be telling the truth or believing to be telling the truth, only they have a line they won't cross. Wait a while, and you'll hear them sharing exciting news about their vacation trip, a new car they bought, or spending on things for which all you needed was 1% of that to survive.

This help may be a token to them, but because we are all made with different mindsets, our actions or inactions are different. Let's face it—some people have built their dignity on lies and low credibility, which attracts no one to help them, especially when it comes to finances. Even when someone decides to help you (we all need shoulders to climb on at some point), for how long would that gesture last?

3. But some, believe it or not, just won't help you even if they have it. A few who may wish to help may still have a limit to their charitable adventure. My advice to you is, no matter what you do, where you find yourself in life, make the most (positively) of yourself and create your pack of freedom.

While we will continue to need one another to climb life's ladder, one also needs to be thinking of how to invest in having the kind of life they would wish to have regardless of their age. The question is, what type of investment do you engage in to have control over time and money? I know quite a few people who have money and wealth but have no time, while others, conversely, have plenty of time but no money. Funny enough, those in the middle who have no money and no time are the busiest of all in life. Sometimes, the best someone can do for you is to give you a 'peanut' of what they truly can do, and you become their slave.

What type of investment or collaborations do you need to invest in to surge and be ahead of the curve? What are you good at? What investment portfolios are you aiming at, and in what institution? Look carefully.

Having control over time and money is not referring to those who rely 100% on their 9-5 job forever. You might need that for a number of years, but you cannot rely on that to achieve the stated aim unless you fall between the 2-3% individuals who are on top of the financial curve, who controls the remaining 90+% in the world. Learn to have cash flow as opposed to cash. The reason is, cash will be depleted, and it can become static if not wisely invested and used; on the other hand, cashflow serves as a pipeline where there is a consistent flow of income.

Consider the following scenario—you're given the opportunity to receive a residual cashflow of $5K per month for the next fifty years with its associated interest (not making it an annuity argument) versus being given another opportunity to receive $1M at a go. Which option will you take, and why? A segment of the population will take the onetime $1M and invest it rather than take the $5K for fifty years with the argument that a bird in the hand is better than two in the bush, and a dollar today is worth a lot more than a dollar in fifty years. A second segment will go for the $5K for the next fifty years because of the constant assurance flow of money that is safe and secured. They might argue this version is wiser because they can reinvest a part of it into different portfolios even if one portfolio fails, the other will be supporting the weak one—which is termed negative relationship investment. You can also freely rely on the remaining and have a target period to work harder and smarter for a harvest day—separating the fruit from the seed analogy.

On the other hand, if you receive the onetime $1M and you do not plan properly, the temptation to use it for short-term gratifications is obvious. That money, if not wisely invested or used, will be depleted, and you'll end up on the streets (mentally and physically). Living within your means is critical. The alternative argument will be someone receiving \$5K a month can also fail to plan properly. In the end, it depends on a number of factors—discipline, good financial judgment, getting expert advice, and being ready to forgo short term gratifications. Look, whichever option or scenario you choose may be better than not taking any action at all—inaction is also action in disguise.

No wonder it is said that most people are interested in making money but are never prepared for or coached on how to manage it. Sometimes you'll need to unlearn certain habits if you want to succeed, by making the right decisions as far as your investment options are concerned.

Learn not to eat your seeds, but rather plant them and wait to enjoy the fruits. In this metaphorical analogy, how do you even determine what part of your income is a seed (in this case, money, for example) to be planted (invested) and what should be harvested (income from the investment) as the fruit? No matter your circumstance, if you can, when you receive income, seek a bit of professional advice on how to manage and spend it. Split your spreadsheet into categories of paying bills, fees, and loans, groceries, taking care of basic needs, a small amount for entertainment once a while (not routine), and then a portion to invest into a long-term fund. A segment of people may argue that a small income isn't enough to invest any. I know this, and I've been there too. But it is only those who sacrifice the short-term pain that wins eventually. There is no wealthy, rich or famous person (except for some of the royals and a few who are born with a golden spoon in their mouth) that got it easy from the beginning.

I urge you to get a copy of my first book, *Synergy and Commonality—The Key to Success,* and read chapters six to eight and see how it describes people who made it and what they had to endure to get there. In chapter eight in particular, there are a few examples of people who were rich but dropped to the floor due to poor financial management and bad decisions—some of whom I adored. If you're busy working and always broke, check in on your life to make some painful adjustments—maybe you're not prioritizing well.

There are bad investments out there, so though I mention investment, the right type of investment has to be interrogated. Do you want short, medium, or long-term? How much investment risk can you tolerate? Consult a certified investment professional who will walk you through the appropriate steps and be ready to pay a fee. Avoid too many free and cheap things as they might come back to bite you.

Ordinary people buy for short-term discounts, while a few percentages of people who think differently buy for value and profits. To them, retirement doesn't depend on the age government institutions decide you should retire, but instead they focus on maintaining an inflow of income for the rest of their lives. They create residual income, thereby separating having cash from having cashflow, differences explained earlier. If you desire to succeed, desire also what it takes to get you there. And when you get there, learn how to sustain that wealth, else it will fly away like a bird.

Spending less on a particular service should not be misunderstood to mean saving. When you go to the shop, for example, and buy a product half the price, do you call it saving? This is what most people call it. You only paid a lesser price for that service. If, however, you take half of what you paid less on and placed it into a fund, then that becomes savings. Most times, we don't recognize the difference to save the money, rather we leave it in our general accounts and spend it. Be wise about your finances going forward and practice this habit of putting money aside. Invest and continue to monitor your investments and review them from time to time, but let it be for the long haul.

Why should retirement be connoted to poverty? Ask the average person after retirement (government regulated retirement) for help—one of the first statements you'll hear is "I wish you came when I was working. Now, I have nothing, no networks, no financial resources or friends to contact for you." This saddens me to hear because retirement should be the time when one gets to enjoy all the spoils of life; travel the world, eat what you want and do what you want at what time you want to do it. It is also that time when you can visit all the sports games you desire, buy the best cars, sleep and rest, go on the best vacations, enjoy your family and the extended ones and just chill out. Why isn't it so for most people? I know people can argue that the average retired person does not have the energy or desire to do all these things. You don't buy a sports car when you are eighty years old and take it to the driving track. You will kill yourself. In fact, with age, people rather tend to view life in more simple terms and become less materialistic. While that may be true, it is also the main reason to have a life full of balance and also not necessarily rely on retirement to be a certain age. Is this age requirement an indication that something went wrong along the way?

Could it be that our government, its policies, or the institutions we die for aren't fair to us, or that we make the wrong investments along the way? For those who are old, my encouragement to you; once you have life, it is not too late to seek late advice for short term remedies to any woes. For those who are in the workforce or working for themselves, it is that time when you need to circumvent any anomalies before it is late. For those who are young and about to enter the workforce, or just started, please, take the right turn. Consult with the experts in the investment industry to begin planning for your future. Do not make the mistake of saying "I have time, let me chill, and later I will think about it." Yes, have fun, but be wise. You can have what the older generation never had; they hoped for a better future, but when they got there, it was too late, or their bones couldn't allow them to do what they wished. So, enjoy, but have an open eye. Start saving for your children's college even before you find yourself a loved one. Start saving towards your retirement with the right fund and make legitimate side investments.

Consider the following to chew on:

- While some wise, wealthy people invest for better gain, sometimes people with limited resources love to entertain all the time. The wealthy entertain as well, but spend their disposal income

- Delayed gratification should be your focus, not the instant ones every time

- Do what most people won't do—that's the distinction between the average and the superior (red versus blue ocean strategy)

- Study the 5% of the wealthiest people before they became wealthy and see why they made it—consider their journey, not just their destination

- Don't let the 'facts' of life dictate your future; work harder and smarter. Whether it be a bad neighborhood, bad environment, low bank accounts, having an accent, bad credit, no connections at higher places, bad schools, immoral parents, depraved upbringing, people looking down on you, people telling you there is no way you will make it in life, having no shelter, no income and many related things—soar above such mediocrity

• Food for thought:

Don't let distractions keep you away from your destiny, because there are many distractions and noises out there. As indicated earlier on, one of the ways to catch a raccoon is to distract it by showing it a shiny object. People know what your distractions or shiny objects are, so they will play on your weakness to put you off-track.

Do you want to consider a second source of income if you need to overcome the short-term challenges to cross that financial bridge? Give yourself a target period to get back in your groove. Some people also invest so much for the future (when is the future anyway?) and never enjoy anything in life in anticipation of a better life when they retire or are old, only to get there and their bones can't take them anywhere to enjoy what they anticipated and worked hard all their years for. Balance your life. Take a moment to go learn how to ride a horse or do something in-between life to engage your happiness— learn to play the piano or roller skate, for example. The excessive use or abuse of such is what leads to poverty.

Worksheet:

What steps will you take to stay ahead of the financial curve for your future? Share about five areas and give a specific timeline.

_____

_____

_____

_____

_____

_____

_____

_____

_____

_____

_____

_____

_____

_____

_____

_____

_____

-21-

DON'T ABUSE YOUR OPPORTUNITIES
—WHAT DO YOU HAVE IN YOUR HANDS?

Consider the following: Talent, skill, education, network, intelligence, an uncle or aunt in a good position, research ability, creativity, capability, using what the land produces naturally versus what we want it to produce (reduction of import but patronizing your local investments, as an example) are some of the essentials we have to tap into. We spend too much energy to get what we don't have rather than using what we have in front of us. We walk and look down on people while climbing to attain the heights we desire only to get there after a few years, and then we look for the contact numbers of those whom we walked on earlier.

A golf ball is only worth the price it is sold for in the market. Still, that same golf ball is worth millions of dollars on the golf clubs of Tiger Woods, Roy Mcllroy, and Annika Sorenstam— and so it is with a Tennis racket in the hands of Roger Federer, Billie Jean King or Serena Williams. The difference is the value they have added to themselves, which reflects on the balls they play with. The ball is less valuable unless someone with great value touches it. The same happens with an ordinary polo shirt—until a well-respected celebrity (like a political figure, sports personality, a movie star or a well-known person in society) autographs it, it is not worth very much. In essence, the value of that polo shirt immediately transforms because of a touch of celebrity on it.

In my first book, I predicted that Tiger Woods was going to come back onto the golf ladder chart —within the same period of the book's launch in 2019, from nowhere (obviously with hard work, persistence, resilience, and focus), Tiger won the 2019 Masters, 15th major to complete an epic comeback. He again became a household name after having been almost forgotten for a number of years. Tiger, like his brilliant competitors, only had a golf club in their hands. That golf club is worth many thousands of dollars, if not millions, because of the hands it is in. What do you have in your hands?

Whenever I see older people who should be in retirement according to federal and government requirements working and competing with very young people at the workplace, mostly doing basic jobs, two things come into mind. Either they love what they do and have decided to stay to keep their brains active, or they missed opportunities presented to them when they were younger and are now reliving their entire life. I will wish to believe it is the former, but, in most cases, it's not, it's the latter—and that saddens me. It could be that decisions didn't go well with them when they were younger, or life did not treat them fairly despite how hard and smart they worked to avoid their current predicament. Whatever the case may be, they should be applauded for taking the step to offset the nemesis that follows them. Let's help them to find fulfillment because they are already going through emotions of not belonging.

When older people find themselves responsibly back to the workforce to make a decent living (regardless of the reason), they must be treated with dignity and respect. They should be allowed to benefit from all equal opportunities that exist in the workplace, such as training, promotion, and other benefits, if they deserve them.

When an opportunity is given to you, it is only open for a short time. Don't blow it. Make the right decisions while you're young, and when you grow, you'll benefit from it—plan your future, invest in your retirement, and make the most of your chances.

What do you have in your hands now? Yes, I mean in your hands, not someone else's. If it is talent, how well are you using your talents to make a difference? Have you stretched it to the maximum or are you using a small fraction of it while thinking that you've maxed it? Imagine how the computer was created. When we see the computer and its evolution in society, we sometimes think it is smarter than us. Yes, it may be more intelligent than you and me, but do you know it was created by a human being? Appreciate your brainpower and talent. The computer didn't create itself, but obeys what it was made to do. Even then, it requires human beings to operate it, and it can only be commanded to do what you ask it to do with precision and accuracy. The fact that you cannot create a computer doesn't mean you're not worth it. Your talent comes in diverse ways. Yours may come in the form of how well you organize things. Others may be great leaders, excellent cooks, drivers, innovators, or team players. Whatever you do, learn to do it well.

Who is clapping for you? When names like Pele, Nelson Mandela, Mahatma Gandhi, Yaa Asantewaa, Aliko Dangote (just to mention a few) are mentioned, what comes to mind? These are names that raise a sense of admiration. We clap for them when they do (or did) what they do (or did) from their field of expertise. So it is when certain companies are mentioned—you immediately associate progress, good institution, persistence, and longevity with their brand. We admire them and clap for them when they do what they do because it is managed well. Who then claps for you, as an individual, a group, or as a company in what you do? Do you clap for yourself? Does your family even recognize what you do, let alone your neighbor, your community, nation, or the world? What impact are you making by influencing the lives of people close to you? We have clapped for people to the extent that our palms are getting stiffened, but no one does that for us. It doesn't have to be something big; it could be as simple as putting a smile on someone's face. How well are you using your opportunities to bless someone? When players like Lionel Messi, Christiano Ronaldo, or my favorite, Ronaldinho (soccer legends) are on the soccer ball, dribbling and displaying all of their antics, people who aren't paid a dime for their achievements get emotional satisfaction from watching them play. That, too, is healing. Whose life are you improving through your skillset and talent? Your time will pass soon, whether you like it or not; whether you believe it or not, you're not immortal, so instead of acting like the moon waits for you before it shines, please consider the limited time you have on earth and make an impact. The irony is, your impact may come back with huge benefits, which basically means getting paid for what you do— why not leverage it positively?

I was in a facility recently for an event. The facilitator was struggling to connect the gadgets to play a sound. These are gadgets he is used to and been successful in utilizing for some time. For some reason, the pictures popped on for a while and then went off. The sounds, however, could not be heard, and this guy was viciously frustrated. He was on this effort for over thirty minutes without success. He called someone to help but wasn't successful. It was not until he called the IT guys to come and assist that the problem was resolved in less than sixty seconds. The sound was clear, and the program went on without a glitch. However, an hour was wasted, which could have been managed if he had just called the right person from the onset. Though we didn't physically clap for the IT guy, we did so in our minds and hearts for this savior at that time. His talent came handy when needed most. To me, he was the superman of that moment.

• Food for thought:

What do you have in your hands? What opportunities are you blind toward that you can leverage positively? Take a moment to ponder opportunities you might have blown past—either because of your attitude, or through ignorance, lack of vision, or less education on what to do at the time—what has been taken by the wind from you?

Worksheet:

Identify the things you have in your hands in terms of opportunities. How can you leverage them so as not to make the mistakes others have made that cost them their joy in life?

_____

_____

_____

_____

_____

_____

What opportunities will you pursue to offset any of the ones you might have missed in the past?

_____

_____

_____

_____

_____

_____

_____

_____

-22-

SEPARATE JOB FROM PROFESSION AND FROM PASSION

Being able to separate profession from passion is as equally crucial as separating that from the job and social environment. Most people work to fill their financial holes but may not be passionate about what they do. The best way to determine if you love your job or not, or if you're in the right profession or not, or if you're called to do what you're doing or not, is this test—when you wake up in the morning, do you complain about that job and continuously struggle to make it work? If so, then you're in the wrong job. As simple as that.

A job on the street—which is called J.O.B, 'just over broke'—is any type of work you do to put food on the table. It may or may not be a career. A profession, otherwise called a career, is what you might have been trained for, something you have spent much time acquiring. It may or may not be something you love or have a passion for per se, but you're good at what you do. Whereas your passion is what you look forward to doing with joy, and you perform related duties with utmost excellence. Let us understand that you can transform your job or profession into a passion over time. It all depends on your mindset and natural giftedness. There are people who at the initial stages do not like what they do, but later, when they grow into it, it becomes a passion. Some factors may account for initial dissatisfaction or boredom at work, such as coworkers, the bosses, toxic work environments, the type of job, expectations not met, a history to the work that brings bad memories, living in a bad relationship which is indirectly affecting job performance, inadequate training, not being appreciated, not being rewarded, not being paid well, not being cared for, or feeling unfulfilled.

You may expect a lot from the workplace or from the hierarchy within your sphere. The question is, what do you offer in return to merit what you seek? Are you also being respectful and delivering enough to attract such opportunities? Do you ask for things in the right manner? Do you give your best efforts to learn? Do you go the extra mile in what you do? Are you always the first to show your back at the door when it is closing time and the last to show your face when work starts? What do you do? Every story has two sides, and I am always careful when it is presented to me.

Some people make a lot more money from their passion than from the profession for which they are trained. Until you find the right dancing shoes for your feet, the floor will be empty without your presence. Until you find the strings to your guitar, your music won't be well played in this one-time life we live in, so find your strings! Let your work become a calling instead of just a job. Having a passion doesn't mean you don't go through stress and disappointments sometimes. You could face daily challenges and frustrations, but what makes the difference is the tenacity, the focus, the desire, and the welcoming spirit that you bring to your task. When you enter an office, the difference in the welcome you receive from the front officers is obvious—some are joyful and on top of their game while others act as though they were forced to sit there and be paid for it.

A friend of mine had an issue with a government agency (the law) and was finding it difficult to resolve it. Even the main agency frustrated him and his wife for years without results.

Since the system was complicated to even staffers, they found it tough to get a solution. Some of the incompetent staff made it even worse. Not until they took the case to an external agency to resolve did the case become hopeful. What was the difference? The executive director in this new agency took over the case herself and was super patient and receptive to every detail. It was a case she and her department had never seen or worked on before, so you can imagine the back and forth—the case required a lot of paperwork, questions and answers, and documents upon documents to prove their innocence. The days went by, the weeks rolled, and the months passed, and they were still working on this case. Never once (at least in their presence, according to my friend) did this new department show disrespect, impatience, or incompetence, in comparison with the previous. They handled and continue to handle the case with passion, respect, and honor, and treated these folks as though they were paying them millions of dollars for their services.

Let me make it clear that, my friend and his wife got the offer of service for free. Or best put, it was paid for by another government agency, and not coming from their personal pockets. The case is almost about to be closed, and as at the time of writing this piece, there is no single regret for collaborating with this new office for their service. This is what I describe as passion and love for what you do.

Instead of asking what you want to be when you grow up (which may be what you are now, or may become self-fulfilling prophecy), why not ask what you will create instead? That way, you are veering towards what you're passionate about, which becomes your career, but comes with a certain sentiment of fulfillment instead of just a title.

Arguably, the type of occupation you pursue and its associated position dictates where you can live, where you eat, where your children can go to school, the kind of house or apartment you can afford to live in, and your general lifestyle— why not make a passion out of what you do? Why not work your way to the top, if that is your destiny? Work as though it is, because you never know; one day, someone will work towards your position as though it is theirs. Also, work as though you're broke, and that's all you have—a sentiment echoed by Tyler Perry in an interview. Work as though all depends on you and pray as though all depends on God—don't mix both as some people do.

Being at the top is not a guarantee of happiness—so my desire for you is to find fulfillment in what you do. No wonder some who stay at the bottom may be much happier than some at the top. It's all about perspective. Working to the top should not be misconstrued with stepping on people to get there. Backbiting your current leaders and talking over them for the evil purpose of taking their positions will only work for a while; soon everyone will see your maliciousness. Just do your part diligently and leave the rest to destiny.

Let's face this fact—when you're in a position rather than your company, you are merely building someone else's dream. You may get paid a lot in salary and bonuses, but it may not be your dream after all. Having said that, if you make passion out of something, you can make that your dream too. This may sound like a double-edged sword, but it all depends on which side the sword is swinging to. It's a combination of skill, long suffering, perseverance, fortitude, determination, support from family, never accepting the norm, being in the right circles at the right time, and a bit of luck that will take you there.

Sometimes working long hours can be demeaning and tiresome. When you get to the point of giving up, take a pause and consider sports like boxing as an example. As an observer, two boxers might be fighting in the eleventh round; punching, dodging, looking exhausted, but not giving up. Meanwhile you get some popcorn, a drink, and then cross your legs, watching these boxers with excitement at the comfort of your couch. You have no clue what they are going through to get to the end.

Regardless, if they can do it, tell yourself, "I too can do it."

To the boxer, that's their way of putting food on the table regardless of inflation. In fact, every year, there is about 3% inflation on average on all products—is that also reflected in your pay/income? What adjustments do you need to make to offset the ever-increasing inflation? Sometimes you'll need to make uncomfortable short-term decisions while aiming at your eventual goal just like the boxer who is almost dying in the ring to survive. Eventually, he/she will be paid well, what about you, and how much?

Be careful what you ask or wish for. When I went to London almost two decades ago to pursue my education, I was excited about the opportunity. I spent the first few weeks touring the city alongside one of my closest friends, with whom I shared many things. On one of such tours was a distant view under the evening sky, near Canary Wharf—one of the most significant business and financial centers of London, basically the Wall Street of London, as I call it. As we were admiring the beauty of lights emerging from the spectacular skyscraper, this friend and I affirmed that we would certainly work in that building one day. We were so sure of it and were very excited because we knew our goal and what such an opportunity meant for us, to be granted student visas to transform our lives. Within three months, we were granted the opportunity to taste the work-life in Canary Wharf. However, the type of job we were offered wasn't what we dreamed about. It was a menial job. That night, I was asked to clean the tall escalators top-down, which took almost a couple of hours for one side to complete and then was rolled to begin the process again. That night was one of the most gruesome and physically demanding moments I had ever succumbed to. I thought I was dying, until I peeped on my friend in a different department with a kind of sweeping mop I had never seen before. It opened like the arm of an eagle, so big and wide, which he was using to mop the floor, sweat pouring down from his face. We spied each other a couple of times during our routines but never said a word, only speaking with our eyes. When it was finally morning, it was as if we had been working three days non-stop.

Our eyes were as red as a flaming fire, or call it burning furnace. We were dizzy and weak as wounded prey about to be devoured by a predator; exhausted to our cores. How we got home was a miracle. I remember, though, seeing young school folks happily climbing the bus and beautifully going to school was like seeing another world to me. Had it not been for my friend who transferred us from one bus to another, with the earlier internal tram from the terminal, there was no way I could have got home safely. That was the end. We never went there again. After a few months, when life began to get better, we couldn't stop laughing over the incident. We still laugh about it to date because what we refused to do was to be specific. We should have been saying we would like to work as chief financial executives at Canary Wharf, not just that we would work there—that was vague. Speak positively to your life and be specific in your request. We got what we asked for. This has become a laughing matter whenever we speak or meet.

Let me make this clear, it is not that we were afraid of hard work or couldn't do it. However, this type of manual and intensive work wasn't born in our bones—or probably, we weren't psyched for it. I respect those who do this for a living for their entire career life. I urge employers to recognize and pay such people well. Value them—my simple plea.

• Food for thought:

Kobe Bryant said in an interview with his former teammate Shaquille O'Neal that finding your passion is vital in your career; but identifying it early is crucial to your motivational soul and success.

Worksheet:

Now that you know the difference between a job, a profession, and a passion, please share your passions and what you'll be doing to achieve them. Also, identify your true profession.

_____

_____

_____

_____

_____

_____

_____

_____

_____

_____

_____

_____

_____

_____

_____

_____

-23-

LEADERSHIP (PART 1)

Two people were working for a supervisor. One finished early and on time, and took some time to relax, refresh, walk around and prepare himself for the next day. On the other hand, the other person struggled to do his job and was not able to work well or finish on time. And so, the supervisor asked the first gentleman to start helping the struggling person to complete his work. On a fair note, it is wise to assist one another for group goals to be achieved. However, after the first gentleman helped the weaker one for a while, he realized the activity had become a routine and expectation. He decided to slow down on his performance, to finish his work at the close of work like everyone else—not early, not late, just enough to not get fired. This way he did not have extra time available to help anyone. Steve 'H', one of my strong advocates and mentors, shared this story during one of the rigorous McKinsey & Company Fellowship clinics.

The moral of the story is much more profound. We do not know what might have happened to the high-performing gentleman who was asked to assist his weaker colleague. Could it be the way the supervisor handled the situation? Did he take the faster person's efficiency for granted, or did he see him as wasting time by taking cardio walks during work hours? It is usually not the 'what' but the 'how' factor in relaying information from leaders that affects the final result and productivity. More than likely, the supervisor did not handle the situation appropriately.

As a leader, you either make an impact, or you don't. Your leadership style could be seen as influencing, demanding, or commanding (rainbow speaking—rainbow was the nickname of an authoritative dad whose words were final, and no one could challenge what he said). It is also true that some people use a combination to achieve the desired result depending on the type of role. Take the military as an example; the use of the command is much more severe and expected than the pampering type. In their case, that is the language, even then, some of the leaders are learning to adopt more mentorship roles than just mere commanding expectations.

What some leaders seem to forget is the fact that they won't be there forever. Twenty years ago, they read about others in a similar position; today it may be about you, but tomorrow it won't be. The legacy you leave behind, the impact made, and how you're remembered are also essential.

Learn to adapt so you can eat with queens and kings—at the same time find yourself in a village and be able to dine with the locals without frowning your face. This is where politicians act the best, however, only every four years, when they need a vote to win a position and so will do anything, come out from their luxurious life and become anybody for a while. This does not apply to every politician, but many know this is true. Their misty car glasses are always shut to the average person until the next four years when they are opened for the need of a vote. This is why some states in America or regions in other parts of the world have declared themselves not to be political vending machines anymore, where politicians come to cash out and go away— and then take the people for granted when they need them most. This is not the kind of leadership I am referring to. They need genuine, caring leadership that they can rely on.

Leaders should separate the professional environment from that of social ambiance. Mostly, subordinates become victims in this case by forgetting who they are in a moment, probably after an invitation by the leader to play a game, watch a movie, attend confidential meetings with them, and the like, because the environment is open. Conversations probably went far the previous day, leading these subordinates to bring up unwarranted topics the following day, expecting laughs with the boss. Leaders should be able to train and manage such people to learn to listen more than speaking and conduct themselves professionally at all times. Yesterday is past; today is a business day. Focus on your work as though nothing happened the previous day unless your boss brings up the topic. Even then, be gentle about engaging and focus on your duties to deliver. This will generate trust and respect for you from your superiors.

I was nominated by Colonel Veronica G. Oswald-Hrutkay in the U.S. Army to join the U.S. Army War Center in Pennsylvania as a member of one of the think tanks representing the private sector. What a privilege it was for me to rub shoulders with senior army officers ranging from Colonels to Generals in rank. We discussed national and global security issues and how countries lead by using the D.I.M.E principle. The D.I.M.E principle stands for the "Diplomacy, Information Technology (cybersecurity), Military, and Economic" principle. The D.I.M.E principle is used to dominate; this is done through diplomacy, in terms of negotiations and related activities. They also could use information technology through superior satellite intelligence and cybersecurity systems to influence or control a country's invasion.

When all fails, they can access their powerful military arsenals to attack any country and interfere with their internal and external security, thus destabilizing the nation if they pose a threat. Using economics is one of the most powerful tools one can imagine. You know, countries sell their birthrights for cheap and bad loans, leaving debt for generations yet to be born to pay for, without allowing these younger generations to be at the negotiation table. That opportunity with the army was an unforgettable experience, sitting at a round table with high powered decision-makers listening to people like us for guidance from private perspective. We were chosen not only because the carefully selected uprising civilian executives were the best brains in the U.S., but also mainly because of our integrity and the fact that we have learned to wash our hands to eat with kings and queens as previously depicted. I was lucky! Always! I learned a lot through the process as well, and will never take that opportunity for granted.

Some leaders never listen but only hear you when you speak. A good leader empathizes beyond hearing from you when you speak. Consider complaining about an aspect of a system not functioning correctly, however, the leader finds it difficult to believe the message, simply because that leader is showered with outstanding services whenever they need them, so belief in the complaint is difficult for them. My caution is for that leader to verify the truth. They can one day disguise themselves to discover the truth. The information may or may not be true, but having a listening ear is critical. Interrogate and assess the truth before jumping to an early conclusion.

Simply put, evaluate the credibility of both the person who is complaining and their sources, and go beyond the surface to listen beyond what you're told. Even if the complaint is valid, ask yourself if it was done in a snap moment leading to the action-reaction—or no action? There are always two sides to every situation when you dig deeper—conduct your due diligence as a leader. It will earn you the necessary respect.

Treating others with dignity and respect should be your hallmark as a leader. It is sometimes a steep hill when people place you in a defense position that makes it challenging to show your true self. Even in such circumstances, stay true to your core belief. This is a special skill one needs to learn and adapt to succeed as a leader. People may make life tough for you, but while you stay true to yourself do not ignore the discipline aspect when it needs to be part of the equation. Even the Supreme Being above the heavens who is loving also disciplines. Such discipline should go with clear communication about why it is necessary. No one likes people who discipline them, mostly in the short run until later when they face some turbulence as adults (not only in age growth but in leadership growth as well), then such discipline turns to become a shining light for them. They will appreciate you eventually, so do not chase the short-term gratification of praise, and stop acting like everyone's savior. Such act I describe as an upside-down humility, which is pride in disguise.

My mom was a strong disciplinarian, obviously with four boys and a girl, she had to be. I wasn't appreciative of such discipline when I was younger until I started having children of my own. Her direction has made me a better person, and I can, with the wholehearted support of my wife, raise my children with careful hands so that they don't compare themselves to anyone. I am still learning every day to be a better husband and person in society as a result of my mom's training. I miss her so much, and it is the reason I solely dedicate this book to her memory. Without her sacrifices, I would not be where I am today. Of course, my dad was our hero as well, very liberal and everyone wanted to be in his presence because he was the yes dad person - who wouldn't want this? But there is something about women and mothers; the tenacity, strength, power and the magic they perform through multi-tasking spirit, woo! Thank you, mothers, and my wife!

It is advisable to note that times are different, so what might have been good in one era may not work in today's world. The good old days may not be a great time today, so beware of that kind of mindset. Leaders should constantly read good books that enhance their leadership dexterities. A good leader should admit faults and address them immediately. Lastly, a good leader should be amenable to changing direction if the current path is not going as planned.

Leaders should not withhold information from their subordinates if it is to help promote the bottom line of the institution or personal relationship. Leaders should also not be scared of sharing information within their span of control. They have to empower their boards, staff, and relations, and create an open-door policy that will eventually help that leader receive grapevine information when needed. This will take confidence from the one sharing critical information with the leader to save the institution. One thing though—while some are rewarded for their confidence in their leadership abundance, others are punished for it. As a supervisor, avoid being biased.

Create an ambiance where people feel comfortable working 'with' you, instead of 'for' you. As a leader, what do you do when people under your control take cigarette breaks (outside of official break times) as an example, and you see nothing wrong with that? On the other hand, when a non-smoker decides to stretch his or her legs outside for a few minutes, it is frowned upon, and they are seen as lazy. This scenario was an occurring practice in one of my previous employment positions, to the extent that one woman who was a non-smoker also had to get a cigarette, light it, hold it and stay outside for ten minutes within every two to three hour timeframe for fairness. She wouldn't smoke it but hold it. Watch your surroundings to make sure everyone is treated fairly—thereby managing crises before they arise. Let the smokers have their time, but that should not be a punishment for non-smokers.

Leadership should not only be seen at the workplace but home as a parent, as an uncle, aunt, niece, nephew, son or daughter—how do you handle what you're entrusted to do with dignity? What is your listening skill like? Are you always in a hurry to speak rather than listen for a while? A good leader listens and analyzes issues before making a decision. Leaders can be found everywhere—in the classrooms, workplaces, on the job, through observation, experimentation, delegating. One needs to pay attention to identify them.

A leader must be strategic in his or her dealings. Get to know the various people you work with or who surround you. There are vultures in human beings, and there are squirrels too. There are eagles and lions. If you're in the vulture or squirrel group, you are a destroyer and seen as someone who takes advantage of the vulnerable in society. Beware of such groups. If you fall into the lion or the eagle group, you are regarded as courageous, successful, and a go-getter—meaning you will soar up high with confidence and will be able to attack any opportunity as it presents itself. I've always liked the animal kingdom and National Geographic programs, especially when I was much younger. I like the way the cheetah, though it is regarded as one of the fastest animals on land, sees prey and doesn't just start chasing it simply because it is fast. It strategizes, moves slowly and carefully, gets closer, and calculates its steps towards its target with precision and accuracy. It only raises its head in the bushes when necessary to analyze its proximity or distance to the prey until it gets close enough to make its move.

Although it is the fastest animal on land, the cheetah also has a weakness—it has only a certain mileage it can go at a time, so it usually conserves its energy so as not to waste it. In that case, the cheetah speeds up and chases the prey until it can pounce and grip the prey and immediately tackles its neck. This is a cautious strategy. Get to know the different types of emerging leaders within your sphere to groom yourself around them. The adoption of style, strategy, and tactics in every situation is key. Did I mention timing is crucial? You can do the right thing at the wrong time. Please, do not hide behind this curtain to delay the progress of other potential leaders—use your two eyes, two ears and one mouth well. They are there for a reason. Use them well.

-24-

LEADERSHIP (PART 2)

The right people are propitious, so for someone to succeed in anything that they do, they have to surround themselves with the right people, and this cannot be overemphasized. Connect with people who are willing and honest. Even when it's not something you want to hear, those who will support and alert you when you're on the wrong path are rare. They will praise you when it is deserved, and they will reprimand you as well when you go wrong.

A good leader removes emotion from their decision-making process. If you add emotions, you'll end up making decisions from your heart instead of it coming from your head. You need the heart always, but that should not precede the wisdom you're endowed to use technically and artistically.

Leadership comes with strategy, success, legacy, lessons, mentoring others to follow in your footsteps, and winning, as well as experiences from your failures. Speaking of failures, I, however, don't get it when in sports, for example, a dominant figure in an older era in the past is beaten. The entire public (supporters) reacts negatively—criticizing and unhappy with the performance of the legend. I just don't get it. Ask yourself if that legend was performing their utmost best at their peak when they came onto the scene, compared to now, and with the fresh, emerging, hungry opponent. Would they be beaten the same way? When Larry Holmes, one of the most respected former heavyweight boxers, defeated (actually punished) Muhammad Ali in what I will call Ali's supposed retirement age, people from Larry's camp jubilated as though they had never seen anything like that before, while Ali's camp felt sad, believing he should have won the match. No way, he couldn't have. His time had passed. In case you don't know, after that gruesome fight, Larry Holmes couldn't celebrate, but wept in his locker room. When asked why he was crying, Larry said he was sad knowing he had demolished his idol in such a humiliating manner, at a time when Ali was no match compared to when he was at his peak. Larry Holmes was only eight years old when he became a diehard supporter of Ali. No wonder Larry, according to Ali, fought the same style as him, moved like him, and mimicked every technique Ali used. Leaders will come and go; when it is your time, do your best to leave the train with dignity if you have any left.

Similarly, when Usain Bolt was beaten in his final tournament, I was sad but wasn't surprised. When I saw how people acted as though the world had come to an end, I was amazed at them. Was he defeated in his peak? Was his record time broken? That should be considered a 'hurray' if that happened. It is like physically fighting with the weak and old person, and feeling proud when you win. I am not taking away the glory of victories from the winners, but it needs to be told that everyone has his or her time on this life's podium. When it is your turn, perform your part and give way. No matter your credentials, wisdom, accreditations or achievements, your time will come to pass. Such accreditations won't save you. Your attitude, performance, and legacy will be remembered more.

There was a leader in a reputable institution who always played golf and tennis, attended events, and who was constantly invited to give speeches at big and small gatherings. She was hardly seen in the office. The board of directors never complained about her activities, but her subordinates were the complainers. Even though the work was going on perfectly and everyone was paid to their satisfaction with huge end of year bonuses, a few still complained about this leader because they didn't see much of her. It wasn't until this leader moved on to another institution that the workers started feeling the pinch—in other words, the company started experiencing downsizing and financial issues. They finally got to know the worth of this leader. What they didn't realize was that this leader, through her golfing, tennis playing and speaking engagements, was using such events to attract investors and signing contracts for the institution, attracting the companies, brands, and stakeholders to opportunities. Though others at the lower end saw it as waste, without her they wouldn't have been paid what they were paid—the company was on her shoulders. Excellent leaders with vision are not always meant to be sitting down like you expect them to. The board of directors and shareholders love the bottom line, they love to see the numbers increase and profitability amassed, so once they were getting what they wanted, they had no issues, except people at the lower end who think everyone should work like them, saw it differently—a big shame.

Sometimes, subordinates complain because they feel as though they are doing the hard work and do not see the value of a leader who understands little and make unwarranted judgments about their activities. Please, wake up from your slumber, you're dozing off. This is in no way defending lazy leaders who enjoy such things and do nothing. The focus is on hard-working, smart leaders who know what they are doing— reason, effective communication, and succession planning counts a lot. Let's face it, if hard work alone is what you need, why then the struggle of long years of education and getting those credentials? If hard work is all you need, I tell you, grave diggers (metaphorically) should be paid more than anyone else. Respect the authority you're placed under and let that authority respect you back. In no time, you'll get there too, and if you're a good one, you'll understand it better when you're at the top so to see what happens below deck—where you used to be.

As a leader, do not judge people's attitudes only by how they play by your playbook or by your strict and micromanaging rules. I have seen situations where a leader wants to follow the company's rules to the dot (which is not a bad thing in the first place) and so refuses to use instincts to make judgments, and as a result offends and demoralizes everyone, even the hard workers. For example, just because someone is late in reporting one minute after a short break should not make you start misbehaving toward that person, especially when that staff member is one of your best. This is not to cover for other lazy staff; someone can be on time and be lazy while another who is late occasionally may be more efficient. So, leaders have to be conscious of that because I guarantee you, if not handled properly, it will affect productivity. As a leader, one needs to be tactical and strategic at the same time. You will lose the moral respect of even the most committed staff if you continue on that path. Don't cook your poor style of leadership blended into a tiny part of a company's rule that favors you, and then use it to lord over your staff and describe staff who complain about it as having a negative attitude. It is the 'how' you approach the scenario, that counts even more than 'what' you intend to do. You can be right ethically and seen as following the strict rules laid down by the institution, while in other ways refusing to use your sound judgment appropriately to lead effectively—leading to moral deprivation and productivity deficiency.

As a leader, avoid what is called 'selective listening,' where you hear what you only want to hear and diminish the rest, where you listen to your favorites but only hear others when they speak. You're fascinated by comments from those whom you like, but easily get irritated by others with whom you don't find a connection. Learn not only to enjoy positive praise or want only to hear what sounds pleasant to your ear, but also learn the habit of accepting criticism as feedback—it is a gift.

A leader should be coherent and precise when giving instructions to their span of control or people who look up to them. You don't only need credentials to be a good leader, and you don't need accolades to be clear. What you need is to be polished and become a better version of yourself, as far as communication is concerned. A leader can choose what to selectively or partially see, but because they are naturally groomed to see only that, the onus is on that leader to be extra vigilant so not to be blindsided. Always attempt to learn from the other version of the story and see beyond what you see alone. The fact that someone has access to a leader and others don't does not mean the one with access' version is always true—interrogate, trust but verify.

Have you noticed that wherever confident and visionary leaders are appointed in any role, they turn out to produce great results by turning the business around? It is a mistake to take a leader out and not replace them with another of the right caliber. Your entire organization will collapse over time. Do not focus on that one negative thing you find in someone to dismiss the hard work of the previous one—soon, you'll begin to see cracks, not because the new leader isn't performing but because their performance will be one-sided, with no innovation and personality attached. The same old way of doing things in the 'good old' 1950s will apply without a focus on the new generation. Such people usually talk about themselves, and anytime you're in their presence, within a few minutes you'll know their achievements and stories because that is all they talk about—watch out for such people.

A leader should leave a positive mark wherever they go. Such trademarks, though, may not be seen in the short-term due to artificial glass over them, however, over time everything will become noticeable. Be patient. Also, the ability to manage the combination of confidence and humility, patience, and composure, sets one leader apart from the other—sets a great leader from just another leader. Leaders know how to place the right person(s) to the right task(s) to create the perfect result for efficiency. Aside from meeting shareholder values, satisfying stakeholder's interests is critical. One of the essential unspoken core duties or traits by a good leader is to inspire—that could be the answer to everything the institution desires to achieve.

• Food for thought:

As a leader, sometimes it is good to be silent and listen. It is believed that sometimes your silence is much more eloquent than any ten thousand words you might speak. It is a skill, learn that too.

Also, when you find yourself in a unique leadership position, do not see yourself or act as though you own the destiny of your span of control—that's how it may feel temporarily, and yes it could be for now, but the coin usually turns one way or the other, it's just a matter of time. Most, if not all of the time, those below you may turn out to become 'big' personalities in society, and you may need their signature for your niece or nephew one day. Your position isn't immortal, and neither are you. Respect and serve as a mentor to help your subordinates to grow—they won't forget you.

Worksheet:

Can you identify your leadership style? What are new things you've learned from this chapter that you intend to adopt?

_____

_____

_____

_____

_____

_____

_____

_____

_____

_____

_____

_____

_____

_____

_____

_____

_____

Share your organization or other leadership perspective you see here, good or bad.

_____

_____

_____

_____

_____

_____

_____

_____

_____

_____

_____

_____

_____

_____

_____

_____

_____

_____

-25-

GRAND STRATEGY MODEL

The term grand strategy is not only used in times of war or at a military circus alone, but it spans across political, corporate, personal, and institutional arenas as well.

A grand strategy is a general term for a broad statement of strategic action. An ambitious and strategic plan means one that is used to achieve long term objectives.

Grand strategy is simply the level at which knowledge and persuasion, or in modern terms, intelligence and diplomacy, interact with military strength to determine outcomes in a world of other countries who also have their own grand strategies.

In the grand strategy model, the average person cannot see the end from the beginning—well, this is the reason it is called so, as in 'grand' and 'strategy.' It is like a good barber who starts cutting someone's hair. Initially, it looks rough and rugged until it is completed with perfection.

It is not only countries or big institutions that have grand strategies, like China, the U.S., European Union, United Nations, or the World Bank as an example, but individuals too can have one. From look of things, nations like China seem to desire to take over the world through one aspect of the D.I.M.E. (details explained in chapter twenty-three), mainly via the 'Economic' means. And so, they have spread all over the world, acquiring businesses, giving loans to governments and supporting industries. There is no such thing as free lunch, as the saying goes. The onus is on such countries and businesses to read the fine lines and the level of relationship they are engaging in, because one thing I know for sure: In the end, their dominance will be seen and felt in a couple of years down the line when probably even the best soccer players will emerge from China. I expect to get dozens of messages from my soccer loving friends to disagree on this assertion. However, should that happen, in that case, everyone will need to adopt Chinese culture to make business life and negotiations easier. The British and Roman empires were the biggest in history, and though not everyone had to speak English or Italian during their reign as global empires, the desire to understand their culture and be able to communicate with them in their language was crucial. It may be the same with China in the future. They may control the world currency and economy and be seen as the new empire, if not already —I am not absolutely confident of this assertion, but it is a possibility.

The above thoughts may be mere speculations, but they are also based on what is going on in the world. Let's also ask ourselves these questions about the Chinese as an example to discuss grand strategy.

Do the Chinese have nationalistic imperial ambitions? Probably not. We are assuming they do, judging from Western experiences, but perhaps the Chinese don't, or best put, may not. China may be Confucian in thought and communist in political organization, but have so far not shown any interest in imposing their ideologies on anyone. Confucianism, at its core, does not promote imperialism, so China becoming an imperial power most likely will only happen when their political system changes to a democracy, which will encourage nationalism and imperialism. A close relation to me put it this way: So far, the Chinese model seems like more of an attempt to build muscles against becoming victims of Japanese and American imperialism. The Chinese felt humiliated by the British and Japanese in the colonial times, and their national agenda is fixated on preventing the repeat of this humiliation. They are building alliances globally to counter American imperialism. Just look at the number of American military bases in Asia around China, and you will understand this much better. They don't want America or any other country to have complete control or leverage over their trading routes, both on the sea and on land.

Whatever the case may be, there used to be other empires that existed, but none have stayed forever. The point is, be it in the 18th century or 21st century, they had and have a grand strategy to deploy. Take a Chinese product for example—though it may be an exaggeration, every product on earth is either imitated or produced by the Chinese. Their prices are competitively low, so everyone buys their products, thereby supporting their grand economic strategy gradually and aggressively. It is a long-term strategy, remember? As at the writing of this book, China may account for just 14% of world exports, versus 9% for the U.S.A. China's manufacturing output may be $2 Trillion (20% of global), versus the U.S.A.'s $1.9 Trillion (18%) in recent times, and they may keep surging. In their 'Marketplace' evening news on February 7th, 2020, K.U.N.C. reported China's economic growth was the third in the world. Whatever the case, they are in the news every day—this is why it is dubbed grand strategy.

The greatest challenge and threat to America and the western world, apart from the Corona Virus (COVID-19) pandemic is China—it's as simple as that. It is rather ironic that this deadly disease is speculated to have emanated from China: Though there is no known maliciousness intended, it still remains the biggest disease threat the world has faced in recent history. Though this has hugely impacted the global economy, other factors present prior to this pandemic, such as terrorism, security, and immigration remain issues but are lesser threats compared to China's dominance of the world's economy. This is because, just as other Kingdoms dominated in the past, China, in their silence, is gradually taking over the world through economic means. I will not be surprised if, twenty to thirty years down the line, the Chinese language will become the lingua franca just as English has today. Whenever you go out to buy cheap tissue paper, or choose a wine glass for its lower price instead of quality (this is not saying their products are always affordable—they just found a way to do business as people are price-sensitive), remember you're contributing gradually to their grand strategy without knowing it.

Quality is no more (for the most part) what is important anymore; instead, people look for what is cheaper and can probably last longer. We are being targeted from the scheme of marketing strategy, and thereby contributing towards someone's or a country's grand strategy to take over the world and its market share in the next century. The average person on the street focuses on what they can afford, and so they care less about a grand strategy but rather surviving in the short-term, considering their budget. This is to provide knowledge about the pattern of how grand strategy works and not to downplay any country or anyone who is pursuing it. After all, that has always been the case for many others. Empires have come and gone, and so will others.

For the individual, one needs a similar strategy to govern their future. To someone watching you pursue a goal that isn't the average person's goal, it may seem like madness initially because you aren't doing the normal things everyone else is doing. Usually, it is in chaos that things get created in the first place. To you, there is wisdom in the madness.

‖‖‖

• Food for thought:

Having a grand strategy is, in other words, having a significant and long-term vision. To the average person, pursuing a grand strategy model seems nonsensical and will take too long until completion. Wait until the masterpiece is completed to see more clearly. What is yours—as an individual, family, friends, community, or as a country?

Worksheet:

What is your grand strategy? What do other people see in you as madness? Is it instead your secret wisdom?

_____

_____

_____

In addition, share your country of origin's grand strategy if you know it (or what you think it is). If in doubt, interview about three people in political leadership positions and compare notes.

_____

_____

_____

Finally, share your organizations grand strategy perspective here.

_____

_____

_____

_____

-26-

LEGACY

There are many ways to leave a legacy in life. It can be through specific action, creativity or through mentorship, as well as many more avenues discussed in this chapter. Let's discuss a few points.

People are placed on earth to guide us, so avail yourself of this unique ecosystem. The reason is mentors also have mentors. Mentees are also mentors to others. There are separate professional mentors and social mentors, and academic or marriage ones. We have different types of such, and so the onus is on you to align the right people with the right needs. Did you know a younger person can be a mentor to an older person in the same institution or community? Mentoring doesn't call for the type of cars you drive, the number of grey hairs on your head, your bank account, or the type of food you eat. It's about the knowledge you have regarding a specific topic area, which leads to the legacy you want to leave. And this knowledge doesn't necessarily have to be fifty years of experience (which is also essential), but it can also come to you in a few years if you pay attention. It is ironic that someone can have twenty years of presence but have zero or only one year experience, while another can have only three years of existence and have thirty years of translatable experience, all due to exposure and the type of environment the person works in and the presence of knowledge.

It all depends on the level of exposure available to that person. Let us not be deceived into misunderstanding this statement. Most people have both the years and the experience, and some other people have few years of presence and will need a lot of more years on the job or life ladder to appreciate the subjective experience that comes with it—no doubt about that. The point is simple: Experience and the kind of impact one makes depends on attention and the broad knowledge that comes with it. You cannot be a mentor and be a narrow-minded person. By the way, it takes humility to be mentored, you need to be coachable and accountable as well, and, as a mentor, you also need to be humble about your offerings. Build the right kind of relationship with your mentee to make the mark you ought to make. Guess what? Your mentee (mostly, if not usually) could soon become the big person whom you can rely on.

In no particular order, below are a few areas one can leave a legacy either professionally or personally:

- Providing excellent ideas all the time—but at the same time learning to be quiet to listen to others share theirs is key
- Mentoring and advising:
  - o Mentors walk with you all through your life. Mentors help you, not to their shoulder level, but to reach your optimum and divine level in life. Mentors tell you what you need to know, listen to you, and do not hesitate to apply wisdom to help you along the way. Advisors are a bit cautious, trying not to hurt your feelings, so they mold you to a path to make your own decision eventually. Whichever it is, that is legacy

- Exit interviews:
  - o When someone decides to leave, or you decide to exit from an institution, interrogating why the person is leaving is equally as important as conducting entry interviews. This concept is super important; through the dialogue, you might find a silent solution to a problem you had tried to solve for a long time, without success
- Leaving behind innovations and creativity for others to improve upon even when you're not around
- Bringing people together as much as you can—be the peacemaker
- Training and delegation opportunities:
  - o Learn to trust people. Allow for genuine mistakes from your span of control to bake them for perfection
- Developing and separating visionaries from leaders and managers, as their roles are different
- Leading by example so others can emulate to become better people in society
- Providing for succession planning—succession planning should not be replaced with being scared that someone will take your job
  - o If you're good at what you do, no one will ever take your job, but if they do, another better opportunity awaits you—you may thank your backbiters later
- Going the extra mile:
  - o Be a 'go-to' person and become the subject matter expert in your field so people can call on you when they need to

A legacy may not be visible in the short term in most cases—not everyone sees clearly what you do at the moment but give it time; they will. Some people live above their age and their generation, so when they speak people vote against them, only to one day realize their vision. Sometimes such a vision may not be realized in the lifetime of the visionary, but eventually it will be realized. My point here is to continue to do what is right. Do not chase the instant glories, instead focus on the goal. Many children, at their tender age, hated and disliked their parents (the good-minded parents) when they were disciplined. It is only when they grow up and start having responsibilities that they grow to understand the rationale behind such discipline and appreciate their parents. I was one. Stay focused.

Oh, by the way, speaking of legacy, one should not only be limited to tangible things, or big things to leave behind or when you leave a place. You can still be present in a position and still leave a legacy, and not only after you retire, die or depart from one place to another. Legacy can also take the form of intangible things, like that simple smile on your face, that confident personality you exude, that reliability in you, that tenacity and power you possess, that joy you have, that positive energy you spread across the environment, and that persistence you demonstrate. The fact that you're happy for someone's success and genuinely promote it can also be a legacy you can leave emotionally and in the minds of people who think otherwise. Those little things you take for granted could be the legacy someone is looking for to move on to the next level. No one remembers your credentials more than the legacy you leave behind. In fact, in most of my career prospects, almost no one asks about my certificates to begin with. Yes, my credentials may open the door initially, but after that, it is all about the legacy.

• **Food for thought:**

Love them or hate them, our hairs rise, and we feel enlightened when we hear names like Muhamad Ali, Dr. Kwame Nkrumah, Martin Luther King Jr, Marilyn Monroe, Bob Marley, Bruce Lee—all from different fields of expertise—due to the legacy they have left behind, and their impacts are still felt to date. What do you have in your hands that you can turn into an inheritance? You may not have the world's stage, but in your small world what are you doing that you will be remembered for? What are you known for so that, when you're not around, you're missed? It is unfortunate that some people are never missed when they are not around. Sometimes it is because of the lazy eggheads and people they surround themselves with. Mostly, it is because they don't want a change or the desire to work extra hard, so such a leader is seen as a 'pusher' or pain to work with. However, some leaders are just a pain to be around with, and so their legacy turns out to be negative—hopefully not the perceived but the real legacy.

Learn from the experts and those who have gone ahead of you and be a better version of yourself. That way, you're able to deliver and perform to your utmost best. Trust and loyalty play a considerable part in the type of legacy you leave. Work on them while you have life.

Worksheet:

What legacy are you leaving behind, be it in your family, workplace, or wherever you find yourself?

_____

_____

_____

_____

_____

_____

What kind of legacy will you leave behind when you leave a place? In fact, how will you be remembered, considering there exist both good and bad legacy?

_____

_____

_____

_____

_____

_____

_____

-27-

COLLABORATION AND RELATABILITY

People may be chasing 100% of nothing both in life and in business and continue to be busy with no results. Consider this, I will instead take 1% of one billion dollars with a 'B' rather than 100% of $1,000. Because of selfish reasons, people walk in this life with individual struggle hoping to make it alone one day all by themselves. Yes, people have made it that way and will continue to make it, but how many are such unique people on earth? I don't blame them, sometimes it is due to the distrust and previous pain they might have gone through with partnerships.

Nevertheless, in carefully chosen and good collaboration, both parties don't always have to see things the same way. What is essential is to have the same goal. As indicated in my first book, let us revisit this scenario in a different context concerning collaboration:

There is an exciting story about the six blind folks and the elephant. The story goes this way: They were blind from birth, so obviously, they had never seen anything before, let alone an elephant. One day, coincidentally, they all had a dream about an elephant, and strangely, they all had different touches on the elephant's body.

The first person declared that an elephant was like a wall. Why? He had fallen against the broad side of the elephant and felt his hand around it. The second laughed and asserted that an elephant couldn't be like a wall.

Instead, it was like a tree, just because he was only able to hold its leg, and so how could it be like a wall? The third blind man laughed at the two friends and professed that an elephant was like a fan because he had held its big open ears, which were flapping. The fourth said, "Guys, you're crazy." He was sad to realize how blind indeed the rest were, and he wanted to let them know what irrational stuff they were talking about. To him, an elephant was like a rope because he had held the tail. The fifth, at this time, was extremely angry because he had held the tusk of the elephant. He burst out, saying an elephant was like a spear. How ignorant the rest were, he thought? At this time, the sixth blind person was fuming as he insisted that an elephant was like a big rough stone. Why? Because this one had held its head. It wasn't long until an older seeing woman named Grace, a.k.a. 'Ogre,' came onto the scene and asked what the issues were. When she was told the story and why they were fighting each other, she buried her head in her hands. Each of the six blind people was eager to know the verdict, believing they were right in their way, based on their senses and what they had individually experienced in the dream. To their disappointment and surprise, 'Ogre' carefully sat them down and told them that each one of them had a piece of the truth. If they had combined all that each had held and described, they would have had a full elephant.

They were stunned and felt stupid. At least it was a big lesson that taught them to learn to listen to each other going forward, especially regarding things they hadn't experienced in their life before. When you think you know it all, someone knows better than you, so you need to merge ideas to arrive at the perfect solution. It is vital to consider other people's opinions and respect them even if you don't like them. If you don't, you may end up jumping well but landing on the wrong foot.

No matter the sport, it could be a volleyball or soccer game, it's a team effort. It takes someone to dribble and it takes another to seek the right person who can connect the ball to the scorer who pounds the ball for victory. Take a piece of straw from a broomstick and use it. It may take you forever to finish before achieving your aim. However, put them together in their bunch and see how quickly you could use that new broom to clean the environment with precision and on time. This is how many people live their lives. They have forgotten that, even if they are the inventor of a vision, it will require other people, either through employment or partnership, for such a vision to spread across the community, the nation, and the world.

For those who see the world as vast and so desire not to have anything to do with their neighbor or let alone say hello when walking in front of them, may it not happen that you fall and need a simple call for an ambulance or need immediate transport to the hospital to be saved. May it not also happen that the next interview door you open for that big breakthrough you've been hoping for, reveals that person you have ignored sitting in front of you. May it not turn out that the very prestigious school you're trying to get your loved ones into, that, that person holds the key to open such doors. May it not happen that, that beautiful car of yours gets stuck somewhere, and your phone battery is dead, and all you need is that person to help you out. May it also not turn out that the big house you live for, which has become your demigod, gets burned, and before you call for help the neighbors would be the people you need to start first aid support. People must learn the skill of humility to live happily. A simple eyebrow indicating 'high' or 'hello' to someone is all you need to sustain a relationship when the need comes—nothing too intimate.

I had an electrical problem at my house one time, and I needed immediate assistance. My house in my native country is situated in a suburban area, where we have a few squatters around because new houses are being built and it is developing very fast. My main electrician lived very far away and could not be reached immediately, so what did I do? I called on one of my trusted neighbors, who then called on an excellent electrician next door to come and help. I had never seen this gentleman before, but when he came, he performed his duties that night and gave me a temporary solution. The following day was a Sunday, and he came back and spent half of the day in the house to complete the work successfully even when I had to leave for an event. When I returned to meet him and asked what his charge was, he was hesitant and didn't want to charge me except for the materials he bought (according to his assertion). I was shocked and asked why. What he told me gave me goosebumps. In paraphrase, he said, "Boss, as for you, we know you very well. Anytime you're driving off, you always stop, roll down your windows to say hello to us as a group, and so we respect you a lot." Woo! The truth is, without suggesting any perfection in me, (of course not), I do my best to be very close to my neighbors, especially those of whom are less fortunate. I sometimes walk around in my neighborhood, and when I visit to say hello to the orange seller next to me, the banana seller isn't left out. On occasion, in what has always been a ritual that my wife and I perform, we provide them with necessary items like oil, rice, and money, and sometimes arrange for meat to be bought for them to share as a community. This exercise is done even if we are not around. My mother-in-law would be the humble servant to do that on our behalf—bless her heart. No wonder the electrician, whom I have never seen before, dragged his feet on giving me a cost. All the same, I paid him as a gentleman, and today, there is nothing I will ask of him that he won't do it for me. Ladies and gentlemen, my credentials wouldn't solve my electrical problems for me. Be humble!

• Food for thought:

Like marriage, learn to adjust to different people and accept them so you can have excellent compatibility. Collaboration is more of a mindset issue, ready to allow people into your space willingly rather than the matter of not finding the right pair. Even those who succeed in a long and happy marriage sometimes have problems, and so it is with collaboration. Make the right choice and stick to your decision, knowing there will always be differences along the way.

Worksheet:

With your understanding of this chapter, what improvements do you intend to make as far as taking advantage of synergy, collaboration, and being relatable are concerned? List a few things.

_____

_____

_____

_____

_____

_____

What won't you do?

_____

_____

_____

_____

_____

_____

_____

-28-

CUSTOMER SERVICE

Customer service is arguably the most essential instrument for your business to get right. Great customer service can overcome poor marketing, but it's incredibly difficult (and expensive) to replace poor customer service with even the most exceptional and "delightful" marketing.

Customer service is beyond bright smiles, getting what the customer desires, and speaking their 'language.' It is also the integrity behind what your offering promises, like after-sales service. This is where most insurance companies fail in keeping their promises, as an example. When it comes to taking money from you, they will do anything and promise anything to get it. However, the opposite happens when it comes to claims. This happens to other shoddy investment institutions as well. At that point, the right customer service reveals itself as not the smiles you got initially, but what the customer is given beyond expectation when they need it most. Time tells whether customer service is genuine or not. It is believed that institutions that keep their customer service consistent in a positive way across the board retain customers over a long period, and such customers stick with them even in difficult times. This leads to increased retention and low turnover, even in a highly competitive environment.

Just as in courtship towards marriage one needs time to confirm one's right partner, in a business partnership time and patience is required to determine the right partnership. Test the waters under challenging times before jumping to the conclusion that company 'A' is an excellent customer service institution. By the way, working with a family member is one of the most dangerous things to do—they all come with their unique challenges, and so it is with customer service.

There are some simple rules surrounding customer service;

- Don't make promises you can't keep— this calls for integrity
- Listen to customer needs and avoid all other 'noises'— this calls for wisdom
- Go the extra mile beyond the standard 'screen trained' effort— customers know it
- Address complaints by the right staff and with high courtesy— this comes with respect and honor
- Do not apologize for everything, but be polite and learn the habit of looking the customer in the eyes to address issues— they know it when you're being 'chickie.' Accept when you go wrong— this is separate from apologizing for everything. In this case, you know you're at fault and you don't want to 'piss off' the customer with too much explanation. Accept, solve, and move on
- Learn to be patient – do not bring your house habits onto the workspace if they are bad
- Listen to the customer instead of hearing them speak. There's a difference— don't be in too much hurry to speak when the customer is explaining something important to you

- Show concern and empathy: Let the customer know you're interested in his or her issue and be empathetic. In fact, be genuine about it
- If you don't have an immediate answer to a customer's complaints, ask if you can get back to them, and make sure you do just that and on time
- If you don't have a clear knowledge of the service, product or subject matter, don't make a fool of yourself—pass it on to the right person to handle
- Treat your customers as gold—in honesty, they are—without them, you have no business
- Don't wait for problems before interacting with your customers
  o Ask questions
  o Know them by name
  o Send short surveys
  o Send personalized thank-you notes and relate with them as individuals and make them feel special
- Move from being reactive to proactive, to avoid crisis management
- Create a community with them—see and treat them like family and make them see the institution as theirs
- Organize award schemes for them yearly and be consistent with them—let it be expected, like the Grammys. Also, give surprises when they least expect it
- Show genuine interest in what they do—knowing it is a chain. If their business succeeds, it has a ripple effect on yours, and the opposite is true
- Let the relationship be mutual, as you see yourselves as partners

It is an ironic thought that those who complain about a particular problem are victims of the same action themselves. They misbehave in their jobs and have a bad attitude towards others. When they enter another environment and the tables turn, where they become a customer, they become the holiest of all and act as though they just came from the moon where everything must be perfect. They will argue with you and pretend as though such an act should never happen. Funny enough, what they are experiencing may not be anything close to what they did to others. Because they know their rights, they use them to the full length with no regard for any consequences to the staff in question. Have you noticed that those who have nothing, when they are out there, act as though the world should bow to them? The goal is not to abuse and manipulate customer service, but rather to use it with positive and with mutual respect for each other, even if they are wrong.

Sometimes the half-educated trigger more problems than those who have it all. This is not classroom education alone, but having half knowledge about a subject matter places you in this category. They want to show how much they know. They talk loud and even go to the extent of being the 'do you know who I am' type of people. Don't be offended if you're in this category. The idea is to help shape your mindset to understand that customer service is a two-way process. The fact that the old saying states, 'the customer is always right' should not be abused. Honestly, I partially disagree with that statement to an extent, but that's for another day. To give a shadow of it, one can be right but wrong, which means that even if the customer is right to complain about an incident or a bad service that they received, or a product that turns out to be the wrong one delivered, the way the customer approaches the complaint will determine if they are right or not. Yes, they might be right about the facts but may be wrong in their approach and in their presentation of it, coupled with the attitude that comes with it.

No matter how good your product or service is, without excellent customer service, you can't succeed to the fullest. Customers can invariably ignore patronizing your offerings due to bad customer service.

One does not need accolades necessarily to be smart enough or to know how to treat customers with courtesy and dignity. Credentials help, as they add value, but that's not all to it. Without customers, there is no business in the first place.

• Food for thought:

Customer retention is more critical and much cheaper than acquiring a new customer multiplied by four. This is because it represents an institutional or personal brand, values, image, mission, goals, and what they stand for. Even when you have a lousy product, customer service can sustain your business until you figure out the right path. People do not just buy products these days, but they buy benefits, they acquire experience, they buy relationships—all of which is customer service in disguise. Therefore, keep it safe and improved at all times.

Also, customers want the truth, and they can forgive you when you share the truth versus covering it up for it to explode later—that will end your business and personal reputation.

Worksheet:

What areas do you think you need to improve in your customer service offerings?

_____

_____

_____

_____

_____

_____

Review the above list after six months to see the effects and amend accordingly. What differences have you identified? Life is always about change and learning to be better. The only constant in life is CHANGE, remember?

_____

_____

_____

_____

_____

_____

_____

-29-

TRUST OUT OF HUMANS

This chapter aims to address how the skillset of human beings is becoming less critical in industries in delivering output as compared to machines—bearing in mind machines won't ask for sick leave, increased salary, maternity/paternity leave or anything that humans demand daily. In retrospect, human beings are needed to create and operate the machines, to perform such work in minutes with the required trust.

Speaking of trust, imagine going to a bank to clear a check and your spouse is at the counter. With confidence, you hand over the check to the clerk (your spouse) for processing. The problem here is that the check was not signed and dated. Will that check go through just because the clerk knows you very well? The answer to this is obvious. It won't go through. Your confidence if not managed properly could be the 'clowns' substitute of intelligence for machines, that are produced by the same humans however being used to manage and control us.

The process has been implemented to avoid human emotions interfering in part with the system that is in place. The process will reject anything that does not fit. Even if the clerk in this situation accepts the unsigned check, she will be queried and might be fired for the oversight.

Ironically, human beings have been put in place to enforce and monitor the adherence of the process, as such, it is in place to protect any human interference or where someone could make a genuine error or purposely want to please another person. The system, therefore, should only serve as a shield to increase efficiency rather than a failsafe solution.

In the same manner, with credentials or not, one needs to punch in their ATM special PIN to get access to their account. There is no way around it.

It's fascinating how humans have been taken out of many shops (especially in the western part of the globe), and they are being replaced mostly with robots, self-serve machines, and AI. In return, at the checkpoints in shops, some of the global chains give out discounts to shoppers, and customers are excited about such offered discounts. While that is good and such technology is increasing speed, what they ignore to their peril is that these industry developments reduce human interaction, reduce human employment, minimize training requirements, and eliminate the need to provide health plans, stock options, and medical assistance because they result in a smaller workforce. The cost savings these companies are accruing as a result of human replacement is so enormous that it could be in the range of 30-50% in most cases. Machines are programmed to be trustworthy and follow a set process, providing an additional level of security and removing human error or deliberate acts of deception against organizations. Machines don't need medical leave from work, they don't need to pick up their children from school or attend parent-teacher association meetings. They won't give the excuse of heavy rain or snow or weather change that mitigate their ability to come into work. These are some of the benefits these institutions see.

These technological developments, driving an increase in efficiency and effectiveness, are creating huge unemployment and leaving both the educated and uneducated bankrupt or homeless. McKinsey research says that up to one-third of U.S.

workers—and 800 million globally—could be displaced by 2030. The researchers found that "60% of occupations have at least 30% of constituent work activities that could be automated…Income polarization could continue in the United States and other advanced economies…"

A while ago, I was lecturing at one major university in Colorado Springs in the U.S. regarding the many technological developments affecting the system, and their potential impact on current and future employment. While this was generally accepted, one student stood up and addressed the often-overlooked point that technological advancement has historically affected many generations in differing forms, and that, while in the short term, this causes discomfort and suffering, we evolve and new opportunities present themselves. My answer was simple. I agreed with her; it will always take humans to create or service such machines, leading to new employment opportunities. But they should note that, instead of hiring fifty people to undertake a role, the impact of AI and technological advancements may mean that the institution will only need to hire five people. It is replacing the remaining forty-five with one or two AI systems. If we extrapolate that across industries, period by period, year after year, rather than focusing on one institution, the potential impact is rather sobering. While this may be conjecture, it is possible in the next five years, and there could be close to a 60 to 80% job cut in the system. Is this our future, one where we are designing our demise in the name of technology?

My intention is not to fear monger. Technological advancements are, in part, the lifeblood of industry progression, but being knowledgeable about the challenges you may face within your career gives you the best opportunity to diversify your skillset and remain relevant to employers. While machines can't be outperformed in precision and efficiency, it is up to you to accept reality and start thinking of innovative ways to stay ahead of the curve. Understanding what the future technological developments may be and being prepared to embrace change by modifying our behavior or careers is essential, so that you and future generations are best placed to reap the benefits of such advancements and turn them to your advantage.

Herein lies the problem. It's easy to be seen as abnormal for not following the herd to make short-term gain and gratification. Don't misunderstand, such a short approach, when sustained and managed properly, may prove to be an investment that secures the future. However, for the majority, this isn't the case; you may temporarily secure a house or have two or three cars in the garage and multiple company benefits, but remember, it is not going to last for the rest of your life, anything can happen. So, hope for the best, but prepare for the worst. Based on policies in certain countries like the U.S., and for example, in my previous employment for some notable international conglomerates, one cannot travel more than six hours airborne without being flown business class. It is a strong recommendation to provide that luxury regardless of your position in the company. Sometimes the temptation of such opportunities becomes so routine that we get addicted to that lifestyle. Even when we are on our own and have to make our personal travel arrangements, we are tempted to travel business class even with our families, as though the company is paying for it. We nag and complain when we aren't able to afford the luxuries we were used to enjoying, or we try to satisfy our egos and buy the lifestyle, only to regret it later. Few can afford such a lifestyle without suffering any financial repercussions, don't get me wrong. I am speaking for the majority who force themselves to live this way and end up spending what should have been invested. They are not able to separate the two. Let's learn to be wise like the ant that stores for hard times.

• Food for thought:

In the end, whether you like it or not, machines or AI advancements have come to stay, and innovations are evolving daily that will become a threat to employment of humans. Identify yourself, know your strengths, and sharpen your 'pen.'

Worksheet:

With the introduction of AI into everyday living, what possible adjustment(s) will you make to stay ahead of the curve?

_____

_____

_____

_____

_____

_____

_____

_____

_____

_____

_____

_____

_____

_____

_____

-30-

THE POWER OF COMMONALITY

This chapter directs its content to the fact that people find things in common with people who share something similar to them more easily than people who do not, and so they are able to relate better and more quickly.

People who share a similar passion, aspiration, or career tend to speak a similar 'language', share similar experiences, and relate at a primal level. It doesn't always have to be positive to find commonality, it could emanate from both ends. What about a group of people who decide to hurt someone? Wrong but so it is. What about folks who are locked in jail together, people on the same flight, parents who have the same sense of humor, people who live in the same community, or attended the same college? People who walk their dogs on the same pathway, come from the same hometown, share a similar education, culture, or profession? There is a common point of connection, good or bad.

While the focus above centered on definite commonality, the reverse, as indicated can also bring individuals together. When two or more people dislike something, that also becomes the basis to connect. Another example is, individuals who don't eat meat or do not wish to see animals treated poorly are more likely to find the same values appealing in another person and form the basis for their connectivity. Likewise, individuals who don't believe in education tend to share a common platform as their ways of thinking cross a similar path.

The power of commonality is far beyond what we like or do together, but it is also what we don't like that can bring people together for a common purpose.

Regardless of someone's background, where they are born, or to whom they were born, we are all one, the same human race—but placed in separate geographical points in the world. Dr. Kwame Nkrumah, the first President of Ghana, once said, "I am not African because I was born in Africa, but because Africa was born in me." I believe what he was trying to infuse is, in part, that certain things are beyond the control of human effort, but whatever comes your way is part of human diversity, which is beautiful and should bring us together.

Relying on each other is crucial to success in life. This is also reflected in the natural ecosystem. The Sequoia Redwood trees, mostly located in California (U.S.), are some of the most significant trees the world has ever seen. One such tree, in particular, named General Sherman, is noted as the largest known living single stem tree on earth! It is 275 feet tall, 25 feet in diameter, and is approximately 2,500 years old. Something that tall and huge is expected to have an incredible root system that goes deep down to stand that tall, right? Sorry to disappoint you, but that is not the case with this tree. The roots only go down six to twelve feet, which is not that deep for such a height of a tree, yet these trees rarely tip over. They can withstand storms, strong winds, earthquakes, fires, and prolonged flooding. How can something that weighs up to 500 tons with such a height remain standing with roots only going down about ten feet? The secret is that its root system is intertwined with the roots of other redwood trees, creating solid connections and support, thereby literally holding each other up. Only redwoods have the strength and ability to support other redwoods. So, beneath the surface, they are preventing the adversaries of life from knocking each other down and providing each other with the nutrients to sustain their growth.

While commonality can be found in similar experiences or societal norms that enable individuals to build relationships, it can also be found where specific skills are held. This is prevalent within industry settings and "pull together" groups who wouldn't ordinarily have come into contact with each other but who create a sense of commonality.

When an institution seeks the right candidate to fill a position, what they are truly looking for beyond the talents and skills is 'fit'—commonality and cultural fit that the candidate possesses with the existing workforce to help him or her succeed in the chosen role. Credentials alone won't help you here, though it will certainly open the initial door for conversation.

• Food for thought:

Commonality may open doors for you, and should be used wisely. However, it is your credibility and integrity that will become the tools that sustain your relationships in the long run—meaning, you need it all.

Worksheet:

With your understanding of the power of commonality, how will you use your network to leverage opportunities that surround you going forward?

_____

_____

_____

_____

_____

_____

_____

_____

_____

_____

_____

_____

_____

_____

_____

–31–

CHARACTER

As one of the stanzas of a poem by my senior brother Menson Richard elucidates, "because the gun is on the monkey, monkey tells you, shooting is bad; however, give him the same weapon and see—he would bathe you in your blood. He would cause a blood bath with the use of it. But when the same gun was trained on him, he had orated that it was wrong to shoot."

The above poem testifies that people use their current circumstances to determine a situation, but when their circumstance changes, their thinking, motives, desires and actions change accordingly.

> *"Nearly, all men can stand adversity, but if you want to test a man's character, give him power."*
>
> *- Abraham Lincoln -*

I was wrong when I said in the past that one could not succeed without character. Some people thrive in life with bad character, and the more you wish bad things upon them, the more they succeed. However, what sort of impact do they leave behind? In retrospect, one cannot succeed righteously without having the right character to back it up. Life is beyond succeeding by yourself without making an impact on the lives of others.

As indicated in my first book, sometimes you need character, not prayer, to get you to the next rung of your life's ladder. I got some backlash from a few who seemed to not understand why I said that, especially from a particular geographic region, but that is even more reason it is true. They only read the initial portion and didn't have the patience to continue before reaching out to me with excitement. Not until they read further did they understand what I meant by that. Some got back again and affirmed that what I said was on point: "Boy, you're right." The simple truth remains; no matter how hard one prays, character has its place and role. This is the strong truth lots of people fail to understand. While prayer (regardless of one's belief) is worthy, it isn't the answer to everything. This was what triggered the initial backslash coming from a particular cultural setting as indicated, and it was apparent in their way of thinking, and so the initial confrontation. The truth hurts, but it is merely the truth. As I stated, sometimes people pray and hope for miracles to happen in their lives, whereas all they may need is character and the right attitude to attain it. How can you be lazy on the job and expect good things to follow you just because you're noble? If you lack a good relationship with people, for example, you may succeed for a while but may hardly be blessed the way you may deserve to be in full. Learn to treat people with courtesy and respect because you don't know who may bless you, even if not necessarily today, perhaps tomorrow. Sometimes that blessing is meant for someone else but through you.

The point is, when used properly, prayer can inform your attitude and can help you become more introspective and shape your character. To succeed, you must focus not only on prayer and dreams but on your attitude and character as well.

Also, sometimes, we are our own enemies. Our attitudes are our destiny killers, I retorted in my first book. Some of you might have been rude to people that might have been divinely positioned to help you but you lost their help. Some were angels in disguise, but because they didn't look as such or dress in that form, we despised them. Some may be keeping malice with their destiny helpers, but do not know. Some may be prevented from achieving something unique, not because they lack talent, but because they lack the right character. Talent is attractive, but I want you to know that while everyone can be talented, character is proof of discipline and of responsibility. Character sustains the attraction talent gives you. Character is a virtue, and sometimes what we call favor is triggered by virtue. In all your aspirations, desire also for a good character; have the right attitude, respect people, and treat them right. Treat strangers with courtesy, and do not look down on anyone. Be kind (I mean 'kind') and leave a positive mark. Your angel won't always be a winged one; anyone can change your life at any point in time. Simply put, though the terms are often used interchangeably, you need a good attitude (character), rather than aptitude, to surge.

Character should not only be seen in the light of good behavior, but also in resilience and the tenacity to respond to adversity. Proving that you are a person of virtue. Great people or teams always find ways to win and succeed—that too is character. It is how you apply it. As an individual, you can score the highest point in basketball history (a game I love), but your team can lose if they don't have the right zeal—this is like winning the battle but losing the war.

If you haven't watched the documentary titled *Together We Rise Miami Heat 2012-2013*, about a game between the Miami

Heat versus the San Antonio Spurs 2012-2013 championship conference epic final series, please do. The Miami Heat needed character and resilience to respond to the almighty San Antonio Spurs team to win. Focus mainly on game six, where the San Antonio Spurs were leading by about five points with 28.2 seconds remaining as they were playing in the home of Miami Heat. The Spurs fans were cheering with white towels, and worst of all, the yellow ropes were brought in by the NBA organizers, as a sign of crowning Spurs as the winners for the championship for that season—the worst sign the home team could ever see, as a commentator described it. The Miami Heat's coach's hands were visibly placed on his head as a sign of, 'it's over!' The home crowd was sitting on a pin, asking for a miracle to happen if there was one. A journey that began 254 days ago was about to be defined. In essence, signs of the end were crystallized in favor of the great San Antonio Spurs team, which featured great players like Tim Duncan, Manu Ginobili, Tony Parker, Kawhi Leonard and the rest. However, in a surprising twist, within seconds, everything changed with LeBron James' 3-point play to resurrect hope for the Miami Heat team. Then, there was an opportunity for Kawhi Leonard from the Spurs team to hold the game through two free throws play, which he missed, and it became a one point game. All of this happened within seconds. In the epic moment, Chris Bosh's block after a missed 3 pointer from LeBron forced the ball to Ray Allen who stepped back into the corner, and with about three defenders on him, made that incredible 3 pointer just before the buzzer, which tied them with the Spurs - sending them to overtime.

Writing about this with the video in front of me brings a chill to my body. Guess what? At that instance, shamefully, the organizers had to send the yellow ropes into the back room not knowing what would happen afterward. The simple reason was, if the Miami Heat wins, that would mean they were going for the finals in game seven, indicating no one would be crowned that night, so it made sense to return the ropes.

I have personally never seen anything like this in my lifetime. Game seven became a reality as a result of Miami Heat's miraculous win of game six during overtime. Ray Allen may be known as one of the best 3-point shooters of all time in modern generation. Still he would be remembered most for that game six buzzer-beating 3-point shot that sent the game into overtime, which then led to the Heat's win in the final game and their championship that season. It was what that 3-pointer meant compared to the many others he shot, Ray Allen affirmed in an interview, indicating that, that 3-pointer shot was the most important shot in his career because of what it meant. This was character on display through resilience. The point in the big story was that had Chris Bosh not fought for the missed shots at the rim initially, to grab the ball fiercely from the opponents to pass it to Ray Allen in the corner, who then made the magic happen, the Miami Heat wouldn't have made it, and in fact, this story wouldn't be written here—it took a team effort by all. After their triumph during the overtime in game six, they went on to win it all in game seven in the home of Miami Heat on Thursday, June 20, 2013. No one predicted this happening after they were down in the final minutes of game six.

Earlier in that same game, one of Miami Heat's playmakers, Mike Miller, lost one of his sneakers during a battle where someone stepped on it. So, he had to play with one sneaker on. Even with one sneaker on, he was able to score a 3-pointer to continue the competitiveness immediately. LeBron also lost his headband through a brutal struggle for the balls at the rim. This was more than a movie. This wasn't about headbands or shoes on, it was about the legacy at stake. Character is all you need, as it reveals itself in adversity. Not to say the Spurs team didn't have the required resilience too; after all, this was a respected, dynamic team that had won the NBA championship for many years with almost the same squad that was playing in this game. But, at epic moments, with a bit of luck, persistence, concentration and not taking anything for granted, in the moment of heat—experience (beyond credentials) and character reveal themselves. "You can never, ever, ever and ever give up," Pat Riley, president of the Miami Heat, said!

• Food for thought:

Character is how you treat people who can't do anything for you. What of those from whom we expect no gain? Would they always matter to us? Character truly reveals itself in times of adversity.

It is also through this same adversity that winners emerge, just like the scenario describing the Miami Heat team above. LeBron James and his team's character and perseverance were tested, and they rose above the challenge to change history forever. This is a guy who is described as a complete player in terms of basketball—dunking, coach on the floor, dribbling, assists, great vision for passing, communicating skills with his eyes to his teammates, shooting (both long and short distances), blocking, steals, clutch play (buzzer winners and on crucial points), average points during games, rebounds, field goals, minutes played during a game and longevity with the NBA—a player who has performed across many different generations and remains great. Also, his strength and athleticism cannot go without being mentioned. Above all, he is a player who always take the high roads. His focus, determination, inspiring zealousness, and the championship in him means that there is only one word that can be used to describe and summarize such a player—character.

Usually, it is unwise to use living people as an example. Still, I cannot go without mentioning Roger Federer, who in his life and in his tennis career is remembered for how calm he could be under pressure—something he had to learn quickly when he started his career. While supporters are on edge seeing him lose to an opponent, the prize winner himself takes things (at least outwardly) coolly, staying calm and only focusing on each point, and he climbs back to win mostly. This is a good lesson to learn about staying in character no matter the circumstances, at least from a sports analogy perspective, and an example from this great man.

Worksheet:

How do you agree or disagree with the statement that one cannot succeed without a good character? Does it matter to have a good character anyway? Explain your answer with clear examples.

_____

_____

_____

_____

_____

_____

_____

What does character mean to you?

_____

_____

_____

_____

_____

_____

_____

-32-

FULFILLMENT (PART 1)

Being fulfilled is a different world to be in. A lot of people are working so hard and may be rewarded very well but are not very satisfied.

Being fulfilled is similar to being passionate about what you do; fulfillment is a total of happiness. You can be passionate about a particular aspect of life but not fulfilled in another. However, being fulfilled is enjoying almost every aspect of life, including family life, work, friends, making an impact and receiving one, enjoying good health, having the right character, appreciating every day as it comes, not complaining, and only having a healthy living.

Fulfillment should not be misunderstood as having money and having high credentials alone. Yes, that is a subset of satisfaction, but some people have everything but are not happy within. This is the reason one should not envy anyone, because everyone's destiny is carved differently and uniquely. Until you know what people are going through, you should never wish to be like anyone else.

In addition to the wealth, the titles, the credentials, and many other things, the desire to give back and make an impact in the lives of others is important. There is nothing more important than putting a smile on someone else's face. Adding value to someone is all you need to make the world a better place to live. Just think about this for a minute; no one takes your paycheck from you, eats your dinner, or shares your wealth with you, so why not be a little generous to society? Make money and put food on the table for your family and loved ones, but when was the last time you did pro-bono work for those who need it most? Think about this for a while.

I came across an affirmation of the things I orate often supported by an article by Wanderlust Worker; below are a few areas I have summarized and amended for you to ponder on. To be fulfilled, learn to exhibit the following:

The habit of gratitude - It offers us a platform for fulfillment. It's easy to want things that you don't have. In our consumption-driven society, we are always lusting after that shiny new object. But true fulfillment resides in appreciating what you have in the here and now. Rather than basing your happiness or fulfillment on the attainment of things alone, base it also on the joy in the process.

Take a moment to count your blessings. Rather than thinking about what you want, appreciate what you have. Write it down. When you write it down, it sends a powerful signal to the subconscious mind. Don't leave it in the realm of abstract thought. Spend a few minutes every single day doing this and turn it into a daily habit.

Balance - While pushing towards your goals, it's easy to lose any sense of balance. Things just seem to fall to the wayside when you're goal-oriented. Even when you're not goal-oriented, and you allow bad habits to do their slow-creep, the important things in life fail to get your attention.

Whether it's bad habits that are holding you back or big goals that are pushing you forward, losing balance is quite easy. Things like family and friends seem to lose your attention when this happens. But there's absolutely no way to feel fulfilled in life without a sense of balance. Think about the things that once made you happy in life and ask yourself why you're not doing those things anymore. Activities which make you happy do not have to cost money all the time. I'm also talking about activities like running along the trail during the sunset or having a cup of coffee with a good friend and chatting about your day or your experiences. Let me add here that you do not let higher positions you acquire in life cause you to ignore your friends or people who were there for you when you needed them most at some point. Also, often simple things make you happier than complex activities.

If you're a creative person and you've lost that sense of passion for the arts, then you need to reconnect with your creativity. Balance is an essential pathway to fulfillment, and you often allow things to go forgotten when you're either too focused on your goals or immersed in one of life's many distractions.

Make a list of the things that you love doing but haven't done in ages. Then decide, right now, on a schedule where you can make time for those pursuits. Even if you feel as though you don't have the time in your schedule, find fifteen minutes where you can do just that. That's all it takes—just fifteen minutes.

Supporting others - Lending a helping hand to others is an essential tool for happiness, which leads to fulfillment. There's a deep and utter sense of accomplishment that comes along with contributing to others. I'm not necessarily talking about having to donate money; I'm talking about giving your time, a resource far more precious than money. You can always make more money, but there's only a limited amount of time that we each have in this world.

Money doesn't buy happiness. However, money, when used to help others, leads to the most fulfillment in life. If you want to feel more fulfilled in life, contribute something to someone else. Use your expertise to help others out there. Not only does this create good karmic energy, but it makes you feel better, internally speaking. It puts your mind at ease, knowing that you helped someone else out there who might not have been able to help themselves.

Pick up a good cause and donate your time to it. Whether it's Habitat for Humanity, The Red Cross, St. Judes, Shriners, or any other local organization around you, contact them and find out how you can contribute your time and resources. Also, you could always head down to your local homeless or aid shelter to put in some time there as well. How about checking within your own neighborhood first? Sometimes we are passionate about things far from us, and we find problems afar versus the ones immediately next to us. Someone hasn't paid his or rent for a while—can you bless them? Someone hasn't eaten a full meal with their little children for a while, and they are looking viciously malnourished—give a helping hand. If someone close by is looking for a job and you can be of assistance, provide it. These and many more are things you can do to make a difference, and they will lead to internal healing and fulfillment for you.

-33-

FULFILLMENT (PART 2)

Tony Robbins, a great American author, once said, "Only those who have learned the power of sincere and selfless contribution experience life's deepest joy: true fulfillment." It's also a great way to instill an element of gratitude in your life. When you help and contribute to others, you learn to appreciate what you have rather than what you don't have or what you want to have. Like any other behavior, a contribution can become habitual. Eventually, over time, your mind can seek out ways to help those around you, and you'll constantly be looking for ways you can give to others in the world. Again, it's not about money; if you can afford to donate money, great. But donating money alone is a bit more self-removed. In addition, donate other unmentioned resources within your means, and it will really put you in touch with what you have to be grateful for and fill your heart with fulfillment at the same time.

Spirit of forgiveness - When you refuse to forgive others for things that have happened in the past, it's one of the surest ways to abandon the fulfilled life. You spend all your mental and emotional energy focused on anger and hate, and you simply forget about the good things that used to exist in that relationship.

When you harbor evil thoughts in your heart for people, it turns out to hurt you even more. The irony is that those that you hurt and refuse to forgive might be living a fulfilling and healthy life and might not be thinking about you in the first place, while you go on hating. This hate and unforgiveness may lead to pain in your heart that could also lead to physical diseases. Although, there are people you need to avoid in order to have a sense of peace in life. If in your heart you mean the avoidance; not hating them, but merely avoiding them, you're good to go. Some people may describe your action as unforgiveness because you aren't communicating or relating the way you used to, but that is their loss. To you, it's just avoidance. Do not let someone's opinion dictate your heart's desires if you are headed in the right direction. Learn to forgive and be free, but this also doesn't mean you eat with them daily. Balancing your thoughts is the key to becoming wise.

Perseverance - One of the surest pathways to living a more fulfilled life is the art of persistence. Even in the face of negativity and people trying to hold you back, you can be more fulfilled in whatever you do as long as you don't give up. My youngest son came back from school, and he was given a prize in the area of perseverance, which is almost synonymous to persistence. When I asked what he did to attain that, he said, "Daddy-Daddy-Daddy," in his usual way of calling me three times, "Do you know what perseverance means?" Then he took me on a lecturing tour; in summary, he went on to tell me it means not giving up on what you do even if it's hard. I was fascinated and amazed by the spirit and focus on which he was educating me. He kept teaching me every day like his other brothers too. It was true! Look, giving up is easy. I know that. We have all fallen short and given up on something one way or the other at some point. It can lead to an immense amount of frustration, stress, anxiety, fear, guilt, and a slew of other emotions.

You need to fight the good fight. No matter how difficult things get. No matter how much stress or anxiety things cause you, push through. You'll be much more fulfilled when you don't give up even if it doesn't go the way you want it to. Fulfillment doesn't always mean success. Sometimes the feeling of attempting something is enough to be fulfilled. The thought of doing good but not having the genuine opportunity to do it is enough, but hopefully you will get the chance to do something when it presents itself.

While you work to be persistent in whatever you do, try not to become a nuisance in the process. You need to add wisdom and art to it. Be tactful and strategic about it. We call it being aggressively patient. Read minds and behaviors, and learn when to push and when to pull, as well as how to use such tools. This is where the sense of art comes into play. While knowledge and wisdom and a combination of skills play a part here, common sense and street smarts play a significant role too. Here too, the 'how' is more important than the 'what' when being persistent.

So, whatever goals you pursue in life, don't give up on them just because you failed once or even many times. All you need to do is push through those failures and keep your eye on the prize. Life isn't all about money and winning at things. Money is just a means to an end. However, you can live a fulfilled life and make money as long as you focus on things like gratitude, balance, contribution, forgiveness, and persistence. Fulfillment is waiting just around the bend for you as long as you can stick to living your life through these very principles. Some people have degrees and credentials and have no manners, and some also have manners and etiquette but no credentials—which is more important? The former or the latter? A balance will make it even better.

The above are words of wisdom that need serious pondering about and also call for attention. More to that, fulfillment also comes with being content, but not to remain complacent. It is just a sign of appreciating what you've achieved at the moment. Celebrate your deliverables that lead to milestones and, eventually, your final goal. Fulfillment is also a combination of having emotional satisfaction and joy for your achievements. Be happy for those who succeed and attain a certain height—that too is fulfillment.

• Food for thought:

Be grateful for the little things that come your way. Being fulfilled isn't only what you gain from your goals, achievements, and inheritance, but also the little things you do for others on the side. Imagine everyone smiling at you genuinely and keeping an eye on your 'investments' because they respect you and know the good heart you possess. Imagine everyone around is protective of your properties because of a repeated but small kindness you show them. One of the best securities to invest in has to do with helping people when you're blessed. Do not wait till you have fortunes to help, rather, start with the little amount you have—it is believed that those who learn the habit of giving a little will also give when they have big opportunities. In the end, define for yourself what makes you happy and fulfilled and pursue it. There's a reason everyone is born, so find your reason.

Worksheet:

Determine the five to seven things that you used to do that made you happy and fulfilled, however, you don't do anymore; probably due to other commitments?

_____

_____

_____

_____

_____

_____

_____

_____

_____

_____

_____

_____

_____

_____

_____

_____

List another five to seven things that you need to do as a way of finding fulfillment regardless of your current situation; be it children, position or other commitments that makes it difficult to make it a reality.

_____

_____

_____

_____

_____

_____

_____

Finally, do you consider fulfillment the way it is portrayed in this chapter as important to you? What does fulfillment mean to you, knowing that we all describe satisfaction differently.

_____

_____

_____

_____

_____

_____

_____

_____

-34-

FINAL FOOD FOR THOUGHT (PART 1) —THE RESEARCH PART

Having and striving for all sorts of credentials, whether you aim for earning academic awards or attaining the highest level in life, is essential. They are the building blocks for other kinds of success. This is why the title for this book is *Beyond the Credentials*. Let no one lie to you. Having those credentials, formally or informally, puts you in a position of respect and honor. It opens doors for you in many ways. It is what you do with such opportunities and credentials that matters. What is essential is adding the various soft skills, which has become the priciest commodity that money cannot buy.

To ascertain my hypothesis throughout this book, I conducted an informal interview in the form of a questionnaire to a few selected groups of people for their views. Groups interviewed span across diverse backgrounds and professions, from different religious beliefs, age groups, diverse ethnicity, family, geographical spread, race, educational background and experience, to mention the least.

Caveat: The result of the survey is personal to the unique group stories, which may not necessarily be evidence for a widespread trend. The result may not have statistically significant value and may not be used to generalize any population. Also, this is not a claim that their stories are proof or indication about a whole group of people. However, their viewpoints added value, provided guidance, and may have an impact on what you think.

The questionnaire went almost like this:

Credentials are essential, and so are academic accolades and awards. Beyond these, what skills do you think are the secret tools that are needed to help someone succeed either in their career path, in life or in their profession?

Various answers received from the interviewees are summarized below.

One said that the most important skills besides credentials include people's skill, vision, a clear purpose that is translatable and big dreams. They also believed that, sufficient articulation of key points in any form of communication—be it open forums, emails, or direct communication—and the ability to tap into other potential skill sets of people to motivate them, are important. One group also emphasized the value of a person filled with empathy. Being able to put yourself in another's shoes and to be compassionate, is a secret tool for working with and understanding others. Another secret tool they identified is being able to get along with others regardless of their viewpoint.

Others continued, identifying determination, self-discipline, and critical thinking as the essential skill set beyond credentials, stating that despite how big the goals or the objectives we want to achieve in our lives are, we need to be conscious that we will face various challenges and hurdles in our life's journey. These challenges are part of the mysterious ways in which the world tests how badly one wants to achieve their set goals. In every moment of our lives, we are continuously exposed to different elements that are capable of triggering different habits or cravings and distracting us from making progress or reaching our objectives. In the journey of life, we are in full control of our fate and what we achieve in our lives and careers—this becomes the ultimate result of our own choices. We can simply define self-discipline as our commitment toward all the goals that we set for ourselves in order to improve and become better. Ultimately, since the beginning of time, humankind has been successful in surviving all the situations we have encountered, and have become the dominant species on Earth, despite our physical and biological limitations. All of this is due to humans' magical capacity of thinking critically to find solutions for extremely complicated problems. Critical thinking gives us the capacity to find ways to improve different situations or to solve problems that once seemed unsolvable.

Other groups of interviewees enumerated that knowing your potential will transform your behavior. Seeking knowledge to achieve your full potential by investing to obtain new knowledge is essential, as well as consistently striving for the best results. You need to be self-motivated to be able to achieve anything in life. No one is a better anchor than yourself.

Another section of people I spoke with infused additional thought-provoking points which invariably align with the above, indicating the following traits for success:

- Having a sense of curiosity -
    o A love for learning; an almost unquenchable thirst for knowledge and truth
- Taking responsibility -
    o Willingness to take responsibility for things more significant than yourself and your family
    o Not waiting for someone to tell you to do anything
- A feeling of culture -
    o Desire to create and maintain thriving, healthy organizations and world cultures

- A willingness to do service -
  - o Strong desire and willingness to help as much as possible in a meaningful way across family, organizations, communities and the world
- A spirit of friendliness -
  - o Treating people with respect and dignity no matter one's position on an organizational board or life
- Productivity as a habit -
  - o Hard work, willingness to get hands dirty and try new things, thereby focusing on what works and tossing items that don't
- Professionalism -
  - o Being as much of an expert as possible in whatever you do and be good at it
- Being seen as someone with potential -
  - o Doing everything possible to achieve your potential and encourage others to do the same
- Possessing the presence of energy -
  - o Paying attention to your energy (physical, mental, emotional and spiritual) and putting out as good a vibration as possible
  - o Also being aware of the energy around you and making appropriate adjustments when necessary to keep energy levels high and harmonious
- Being seen as inspirational -
  - o Someone who is inspiring, who trains the next generation through succession planning, instead of maintaining job security by keeping all to oneself

To wrap up on the interviewees, a respectable individual opened my eyes to something I never knew about her until a long conversation we had at the dinner table. She was a former colleague from my previous life in the corporate world. We've known each other over a decade. She used her personal story to demonstrate how someone with zero degrees has attained greatness in her career and inspired thousands of people in her career path. She wasn't telling me to downplay education in any way, but only as a testimony that everything you put your mind to can be possible, regardless. As she put it, she had angels along her life's path that trusted in her, believed in her capabilities, and provided training opportunities to her from the onset, at the early age of eighteen years, and these have become the tools that guided her towards more significant jobs. These people saw potential in her that she never knew she had. Today, she is at the upper echelon of a major tech company, leading, managing, and making high powered decisions that affect the globe and our day to day living. However, she did not make it there without on the job training and paying attention to details. No one wants to let her go because she is smart, intelligent, and loves people, and until you are told, you would never guess that she does not possess a single degree.

It was fascinating to receive a unanimous response from these uniquely selected groups of interviewees whose stories relate to each other despite coming from separate environments, experiences, and age groups. I summarize the interviewees' assertions in the statement that, regardless of what someone possesses, they still need a strong will to achieve anything significant in this life.

-35-

FINAL FOOD FOR THOUGHT (PART 2) —THE CONCLUSION

Credentials have their place—it has personally opened so many doors for me even before people paid attention to my capabilities. One cannot deny the power and impact of credentials when you have them.

While education is important, training is critical. We need to turn education into training instead of just sitting down for so many years in a classroom, seeking degrees which may or may not be connected to the industry in which we seek to work, or to our future competition and financial freedom.

At a point in your life (professionally or personally), you're bound to experience some delays and challenges. In the midst of that, make sure to find the best solution or short-term alternative(s) while you keep your eyes on the long-term goal. Keep moving forward and don't sleep away your vison, because delays won't wait for you.

Education and credentials are a necessary evil to have. Still, so much emphasis has been put on the phrase, "Go to school, get an education, get trained, acquire certificates and degrees, and get a good job in the future." Hardly ever do people ask what your passion is—which will determine the correct path to take to achieve it. While education or training is good, we also end up pounding so much debt in student loans and sometimes, not using the certificates we acquire for their intended purpose. Less has been said about creativity and personal development. Having both will place you on top of the curve regarding anything you do, for sure. The days of having secured jobs or being in jobs that last for forty or fifty years have become a thing of the past. There are disruptions and disruptors which create uncertainties and the need always to have alternative plans. This is not to suggest that you should not be faithful or loyal in your workplace; continue to do your utmost best and be faithful to your task, but the truth is when the day comes when you're no longer needed because of a disruption, the institution won't be shy to let you go. This is the hard truth and more of an awareness message.

Be careful about judging someone's intelligence just by the way they speak, sound, and look. The fact that someone isn't articulating his or her views in a way that is familiar to you; for example, not exhibiting "I" correctly in your language or dialect does not define their intelligence. Someone could be articulate but not intelligent. Given a choice between articulation and coherency, I will go for the latter, though it certainly depends on the need at the time. If you need someone to give a public lecture without questions from the audience, someone who articulates may be better. The point explains itself; look beyond the initial looks. Having both will make it the best-case scenario.

English isn't the basis for intelligence. Imagine working in an Arabic country, and all you can speak is English—does that mean you don't know your job, merely because you can't speak Arabic? No, unless the job requires constant communication with the locals, this does not mean not being efficient. Same goes with every language or dialect. Let's go beyond language to knowledge and skill set. Know that beyond talents and skills, awards and accolades lie the values of honor, integrity, credibility, and the treatment of other people with respect and dignity.

Education and training are effective when you add non-technical values as well as other critical elements mentioned in this book to your life. After all, I have spent several years, money, time, and energy, as well as tossing between opportunity costs along the way to acquire degrees across the globe from various disciplines. This has created and continues to open doors for me. Credentials certainly made a difference and helped, but that's not the point. The point remains that, without sharpening my natural personality—and, to be fair, receiving some luck along my life's journey—I wouldn't be where I am now.

Given this, my wife and I always spent the time to educate our boys on the non-academic but necessary skills that they need to possess if they want to succeed in life—things like ethical values, good manners, and respect, regardless of someone's orientation, culture or religious beliefs. We continue to teach them other critical things like acquiring honor, integrity, credibility, humility (not the upside-down style), faith, good morals, accountability—taking ownership when wrong. We taught them to apologize when they are wrong, but remain mentally healthy and tough on the path towards achieving their vision—not allowing anyone to bully and disrespect them or to take their values to mean weakness. We also teach them to give back and be kind, but use common sense all the time. These skills and many others, we believe, when added to their God-given and personal dreams, will help them not only succeed in life but be fulfilled.

Evaluate this: How many top executives, C.E.O.s, presidents of large and small institutions, or inventors were necessarily first-class students? That is, if they attended college or completed it in the first place, just to say the least! The simple point is, there is more to life and success than just fighting for ONLY credentials. Such credentials, if not attained well, could become hollow and void. Have you ever seen someone, well-educated and sharp in their previous life who is living under intense poverty and going around begging for alms? Not to say success or fulfillment is directly proportional to wealth, but you can't also live your entire life with all the credentials but not be able to feed yourself or family—such credentials become worthless. This does not include those who go through short-term challenges in order to surge. We all do.

Having mental and emotional strength coupled with knowledge, talent, network, wisdom, credentials (yes, credentials), exposure, and street smarts could catapult you to the top in your endeavor. In the same way, it is believed that to succeed and rise to the top in a business office setting, for example, about 15% will depend on how people perceive you, 35% is about what you do, and 50% relies on the relationship you have with people and with your superiors—this is what allows your credentials to shine.

Don't be deceived; at the end of the day, titles and credentials certainly add value to your career. These values can be tangible or intangible. It is what you do with your education that matters, instead of chasing titles and credentials alone. Many people have dozens of certificates and credentials; however, some of them have no real knowledge. Others have the practical knowledge but no certificate or credentials to back it. Knowledge is powerful. Sometimes it takes experience to acquire it—seek it!

FINAL WORKSHEET

After reading all chapters of this book, what stood out to you? Write your take-aways and share them with the author at info@evansmensah.com and title your message "Feedback on Reading *Beyond the Credentials*."

All worksheets can be downloaded at

http://evansmensah.com/btcworksheets

_____

_____

_____

_____

_____

_____

_____

_____

_____

_____

_____

_____

CALL TO ACTION

To support the author's journey with his youth empowerment seminars and other social impact events across the globe, please use the following means:

PayPal ID: info@diversifyingourcommunities.org; Name: Diversifying Our Communities

Visit his website on www.evansmensah.com for further ways to reach the author with your support.

Follow him at his social media handles:

@EvansKwesiMens1

https://www.facebook.com/emensah81

https://www.instagram.com/evanskwesimensah/

https://www.linkedin.com/in/evansmensah/

Thank you!

ABOUT THE AUTHOR
- EVANS KWESI MENSAH (A.K.A. SELORM)

Evans is an educator, an investigative and accidental bestselling author. A trained McKinsey & Company Fellow and expert on organizational development and transformational leadership. A trio continental executive leader with Fortune 500 companies across North America, Europe, and Africa. Evans currently serves as a strategy consultant to many companies and a personal coach to top executives. He is the past national council member for the United Nations Association for U.S.A. and the first chair for the collaborations and partnership committee, SDG 17. He is also the country committee chair for the Dwight Eisenhower Fellowship in Ghana. Evans serves on many boards, including the Howard University School of Business Executive Education and Center for Career Excellence (he chairs the committee on

Career Excellence) in Washington D.C. Evans was privileged to have also served in a private citizen think-tank at the U.S. Army War Center on national and global security issues in Pennsylvania, U.S.A.

He is a certified lean 6 sigma black belt, and the executive director and co-founder of ValueCycle LLC., a Supply Chain Management, training, educational and best practice institution.

He is happily married to Baake, the architect of his vision, and they are blessed with three amazing boys: Selorm Evans Jr. (a.k.a. SJ), Selassie Ethan (a.k.a. Papa E), and Sena Eamonn (a.k.a. Gergeh). Call them thirty children in three. These are his rock stars! More on Evans' journey, achievements, social impact endeavors and others can be found on: http://www.evansmensah.com.

This book was sponsored by the North America branch of ValueCycle LLC

Website: www.valuecyclelimited.com

Author's previous bestselling book: